MESSAGES

Interpersonal

Models

Non-Verbal

Language

Myth

James Bond

Media

Genres

Semiotics

Jokes

Images

SIGNS

In memory of Floyd Horowitz

MESSAGES

An Introduction to Communication

Arthur Asa Berger

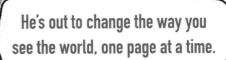

He's out to change the way you see the world, one page at a time.

Capitalist pig.

Left Coast Press Inc.

Walnut Creek, California

LEFT COAST PRESS, INC.
1630 North Main Street, #400
Walnut Creek, CA 94596
http://www.LCoastPress.com

Copyright © 2015 by Left Coast Press, Inc.

All rights reserved. No part of this publication may be reproduced, stored in a retrieval system, or transmitted in any form or by any means, electronic, mechanical, photocopying, recording, or otherwise, without the prior permission of the publisher.

ISBN 978-1-61132-900-1 paperback
ISBN 978-1-61132-902-5 consumer eBook

Library of Congress Cataloging-in-Publication Data on file.

Printed in the United States of America

∞™ The paper used in this publication meets the minimum requirements of American National Standard for Information Sciences—Permanence of Paper for Printed Library Materials, ANSI/NISO Z39.48–1992.

Left Coast Press, Inc. is committed to preserving ancient forests and natural resources. We elected to print this title on 30% post consumer recycled paper, processed chlorine free. As a result, for this printing, we have saved:

4 Trees (40' tall and 6-8" diameter)
2 Million BTUs of Total Energy
399 Pounds of Greenhouse Gases
2,164 Gallons of Wastewater
145 Pounds of Solid Waste

Left Coast Press, Inc. made this paper choice because our printer, Thomson-Shore, Inc., is a member of Green Press Initiative, a nonprofit program dedicated to supporting authors, publishers, and suppliers in their efforts to reduce their use of fiber obtained from endangered forests.

For more information, visit www.greenpressinitiative.org

Environmental impact estimates were made using the Environmental Defense Paper Calculator. For more information visit: www.papercalculator.org.

CONTENTS

One page at a time...

ACKNOWLEDGMENTS

I would like to thank Mitch Allen for suggesting I write this book, for his suggestions about how the book might be organized, and his comments, all through the drafts, about enhancements to the discussions that might be considered. I also want to thank all the communication scholars and theorists whose work I have used in the book. I also owe a debt of gratitude to my production editor Ryan Harris, copy editor Michael Jennings, my book designer Hannah Jennings, and everyone else involved in the production of this book. It takes a number of people to produce a book, and I appreciate the efforts of everyone who worked on it. I've used a number of my own drawings and other images to make the book more visually interesting and have drawn upon my previous writings in updated versions at various places in this book.

Introduction

Changing the Way You See the World, One Page at a Time

The medium Is the message.

Interpersonal
Models
Non-Verbal
Language
Myth
James Bond
Media
Genres
Semiotics
Jokes
Images
SIGNS

What would Freud say? Marx? Saussure?

Messages: An Introduction to Communication by Arthur Asa Berger, 10–15.

Rhetoric does certain things; it has certain *functions*. In its broadest sense, rhetoric refers to the ways in which **signs** influence people; and through that influence, rhetoric makes things happen. When people speak, when they make television advertisements, when they write essays, they are attempting to carry out some function. What that function specifically is, whether it is good or bad, will vary with one's definition. The Sophists would say that the function of rhetoric is to persuade others while participating in a democratic society, while Plato would say that the function of rhetoric is to flatter or mislead people.

Barry Brummett, *Rhetoric in Popular Culture,* 3rd Edition

At this moment he wished to be a man without qualities. But this is probably not so different from what other people sometimes feel too. After all, by the time they have reached the middle of their life's journey few people remember how they have managed to arrive at themselves, at their amusements, their point of view, their wife, character, occupation and successes, but they cannot help feeling that not much is likely to change any more. It might even be asserted that they have been cheated, for one can nowhere discover any sufficient reason for everything's having come about as it has. It might just as well have turned out differently. The events of people's lives have, after all, only to the least degree originated in them, having generally depended on all sorts of circumstances such as the moods, the life or death of quite different people, and have, as it were, only at the given point of time come hurrying towards them. Something has had its way with them like a flypaper with a fly; it has caught them fast, here catching a little hair, there hampering their movements, and has gradually enveloped them, until they lie, buried under a thick coating that has only the remotest resemblance to their original shape.

Robert Musil, *The Man Without Qualities*

Like all authors, I'd like to think that this book will change the way you think about its subject—in this case, **communication.** And I hope it will also change the way you see the world and maybe even change, to some degree, how you think about yourself.

Inside every fat book there is a thin book struggling to escape. This book is a thin book that has escaped from being a fat book by focusing upon what I believe to be the key **concepts** or most important elements in the communication process, such as words, **conversation**, rhetoric, **codes**, **language**, methods of analysis, textual criticism, and visual communication.

A number of years ago an editor asked me to write an introduction to communication. "Write one for me and you'll be able to take your wife to Europe every summer," he said. As we spoke, the **image** of a big, fat book formed in my mind, and I declined his offer. You have to understand that it is very difficult for a writer to decline an offer to publish a book by an editor, because the idea of being able to take one's wife to Europe every summer is powerful. I declined because I realized that I wasn't the kind of person to write one of those gigantic introductions to communication, as most editors envision such books.

I used a football **metaphor** to explain why I didn't want to write the book. "You want a fullback kind of writer," I said, "a big, strong bruiser of a writer who can easily crank out a thousand or fifteen hundred pages of manuscript. I am more like a wide receiver, and like all wide receivers, I am guided by my own passions. I write short books on topics that interest me." That was twenty years ago.

So, when Mitch Allen and I were having a nice dim sum lunch at the House of Banquet Restaurant on Clement Street

in San Francisco and he suggested I write an introduction to communication, I accepted his offer because I realized that he would let me write a different kind of introduction to communication than the usual ones. And because having been rejected so many times by Allen, who I call "The Great Rejecter," the idea of not accepting his request that I write a book didn't enter my mind. He also wanted a book of about 50,000 words—a relatively moderate sized book as introductions to communication books go.

I decided to focus upon *messages* and the various ways in which we generate messages and others interpret them. I argue that we are always sending messages, even though we may not be conscious of doing so; we are always receiving messages from others who may not realize they are sending them, and we all try to control the messages we send to others and interpret the messages we receive from them to the best of our ability.

The term "communication" covers a lot of territory. We find communication in conversations, in debates, in courses on rhetoric and argumentation, in fashion, in advertising, in **mass** mediated **texts**, in **facial expressions**, in **body language**, in texts we read, in television programs we watch, in films we see, and in all kinds of things we gaze at on our smartphones and tablets. Even when we say or do nothing—especially when a response is expected—we are communicating. My point is—we are always communicating; we are always sending and receiving messages.

Contemporary communication departments didn't exist in universities three decades ago. They have been constructed from a variety of other departments in the university—rhetoric and public speaking, speech therapy, mass media, social psychology, broadcasting, journalism, advertising, and others. So, now when you take the basic course in communication, you get a slice of many of these topics to explore the dimensions of the field. This book is no exception, a brief introduction to the many pieces of the field of communication.

Because he is so familiar to filmgoers, I use the fictional character James Bond, created by novelist Ian Fleming and many different movie producers, as a subject for analysis and discussion throughout this book—and, in particular, I focus upon Fleming's *Dr. No,* his fifth novel and the first of his novels to be made into a film, in 1962.

It is my practice to make extensive use of quotations from important thinkers, so you can see not only what they said but also how they expressed themselves. Thus, if you think some concept is hard to accept, such as Freud's Oedipus complex, you might change your mind after reading what Freud himself had to say about it. The Oedipus complex—broadly speaking, a powerful attachment that young children have to the parent of the opposite sex and jealousy of the parent of the same sex, which can lead to psychological problems if not resolved—will be discussed in more detail later in the book.

To help the learning process, I have added a number of my drawings and other images to make the book more visually engaging. I also offer "applications" at the end of each chapter that will make you think about what you've read and help you apply some of the concepts you have learned. In these applications I suggest topics for research, provide quotations to be discussed, and do a number of other things to help you move from learning about a theory and its concepts—for example, **psychoanalytic theory** and the Oedipus complex—to getting a better idea of their **role** in the communication process and how they function in society.

After reading this book you will have learned a great deal about the communication process and what thinkers, such as **Aristotle**, Sigmund Freud, Karl Marx, Ferdinand de Saussure, Charles S. Peirce, Vladimir Propp, Bruno Bettelheim, Claude Lévi-Strauss, **Basil Bernstein**, Roman Jakobson, **Marshall McLuhan** and Clotaire Rapaille (most of these names may not be familiar to you), had to say about various aspects of communication. You will learn methods that you can apply to communication and media and to your life that will help you see the world differently.

A few years ago, I was shopping in a supermarket and a woman came up to me. "Dr. Berger," she said. "Good to see you again. Do you remember me? I took your course on media criticism twenty years ago. What I learned about semiotics and other theories," she said, "do you know—*they are still with me.*" I would like to hope that what you learn from this book will be with you for a long time and will help you understand better the role communication plays in society and in your life. That's because while *Messages* is about communication as a subject to be studied, it is also about the role communication plays in your life.

Applications

1. Investigate scholarly studies of the James Bond phenomenon. What do reviewers say about his books and the James Bond films? What differences do you find between scholarly articles on Bond and the Bond films and articles and reviews of the Bond films in popular newspapers and magazines? How do writers explain Bond's popularity?

2. Read what Freud wrote about the Oedipus Complex (www. cla.purdue.edu/.../Oedipus). Then, do some research on what more contemporary psychologists have written on this topic. Is the Oedipus Complex universal—as Freudians claim?

3. What do you think about Musil's ideas, expressed in the quotation at the beginning of the chapter? Was he a pessimist or a realist?

Chapter 1

Theories of Communication

Messages: An Introduction to Communication by Arthur Asa Berger, 16–33.

Though communication is certainly a tool for conducting the everyday business of our lives, it is also at the core of who we are, what we think, and what we do. The debate over whether communication reflects or creates the reality we call our lives oversimplifies the relationship between communication and the things about which we communicate…. Our communication reflects the world within and around us, and simultaneously creates it. For now, "symbols shape meaning" is a phrase that best captures the idea that communication gives meaning to reality, whether reality is an object in the physical world or an idea in our minds. Imagining the meaning of any pre-existing thing or thought in this world, untouched by communication, is difficult…. In short, communication plays a significant role in who we are, what we know, and what we do.

> Jodi R. Cohen, *Communication Criticism: Developing Your Critical Powers*

There is no "mass" communication because there is no "mass" audience. Instead, there are many audiences, some with structures and leadership and others without these characteristics. Some audiences last only a few hours (Super-bowl viewers) while others last for a whole season (diehard football fans). Some audiences are based on a need for immediate information (viewers of CNN), some on in-depth information (readers of news magazines), some on a need for a religious experience (viewers of the PTL Club), some on a need for political stimulation, musical entertainment, romantic fantasy, and on and on… Each of us is a member of multiple audiences.

> W. James Potter, *Media Literacy*

Communication, Jodi Cohen suggests, is central to being human. It is through one or another means of communication—words we use, our facial expressions, our body language, works of art we create, and so on—that we reveal our emotions, learn things, teach things to others, and relate in complicated ways to other human beings and to society. In modern times, we communicate en masse with large groups of people through various physical and electronic media as well as in person. It has been estimated that we speak around 16,000 words a day (abcnews.go.com/Technology/story?id=3348076)—though we repeat many of the words we use, so we don't use that many different words. Some of you may send 100 text messages a day to friends, which adds up to around 3,000 text messages a month and 36,000 text messages a year.

One reason the smartphone has assumed such an important role in our lives is that these devices, which are powerful mini-computers, enable us to communicate with others, and connecting with others is of great importance to us, for we are social animals. Being connected with others is so important that large numbers of young people now sleep with their mobiles next to them.

Defining Communication

This book is an introduction to the study of communication and covers everything from talking to oneself to the impact of the mass media on individuals and society. I begin by defining communication. Or trying to define it, because there are many different definitions of communication, explanations of the communication process, and ways of understanding communication. McQuail and Windhal list definitions in *Communication Models for the Study of Mass Communication*:

> The transmission of information, ideas, attitudes, or emotion from one person or group to another (or others) primarily through symbols. (Theodorson and Theodorson 1969)

> In the most general sense, we have communication wherever one system, a source, influences another, the destination, by manipulation of alternative symbols, which can be transmitted over the channel connecting them. (Osgood et al. 1957)

Communication may be defined as "social interaction through messages." (Gerbner, 1967)

McQuail and Windahl then offer their own definition of communication (1993:5).

Thus, in the most general terms, communication involves a sender, a channel, a message, a receiver, a relationship between sender and receiver, an effect, a context in which communication occurs and a range of things to which "messages" refer....Communication can be any or all of the following: an *action on* others; an *interaction with* others and a *reaction to* others.

Marcel Danesi, a semiotician, defines communication in his book *Understanding Media Semiotics* (2002:220) as follows:

Social interaction through messages; the production and exchange of messages and meanings; the use of specific modes and media to transmit messages.

These definitions have a common theme: It is messages that people send back and forth to one another that are central to the communication process, and, I suggest, it is **semiotics**, the science of signs and the rules by which we send messages and find meaning in those sent by others, that informs this definition. We will discuss semiotics in Chapter 3.

The term "communication" comes from a Latin term *communicatus* that means "to make known, to make common." Communication has, as its root, the word "community," because communities are groups of people held together by communication, among other things. Thus, communication involves the transmission of

messages, of one kind or another, to others—a person, a **small group** of people, or a large number of people via mass media. The term in plural—"communications"—refers to *what* we communicate, that is, to the messages we send to one another.

As I suggested earlier, we communicate in many ways, such as by voice, touch, facial expression, body language, works of art, and words. We see, then, that some of our communication is verbal and some is non-verbal. It is important that the messages we send are understood and interpreted correctly by those to whom we send them. This is not always the case. For example, if we write in an awkward manner, our readers will find it difficult to understand what we are trying to say. People may also interpret our facial expressions incorrectly. Some communication scholars argue that decoding communication aberrantly is the norm.

Communication is studied in many different departments in universities. At San Francisco State University, where I taught for many years, there were two communication departments: one was Speech Communication, and involved courses on rhetoric, **public speaking**, argumentation and that kind of thing. I taught in the **Broadcast** and Electronic Communication Arts department, which offered courses on media criticism, media aesthetics, and media ethics and studio courses on sound, radio, television, and new technologies. But communication is also studied in English departments, political science departments, psychology departments, film departments, business departments, and many other departments in a typical university. And written communication, in the form of essays and term papers and reports, is in every department.

Models of the Communication Process

To get an insight into how communication works, I offer here a few well known **models** of the communication process. Models show the elements in some phenomenon and the relationship that exists between these elements. We often find diagrams in models that show how the elements relate to one another. This is because our eyes can often see relationships very quickly. **Theory** can often be very abstract, so these models should help you understand how previous scholars have viewed the field.

Aristotle's Model of the Persuasion Process

At one time the sub discipline of communication called *rhetoric* was confined to the
study of speech and persuasion—which is
what Aristotle writes about—but nowadays
it deals with all kinds of communication,
such as analyzing great speeches, classic novels, great films, and works of the mass media
and **popular culture**. For example, there is a
book, *Rhetoric in Popular Culture*, by Barry
Grummet, published in 2006, that used rhetorical approaches to analyze popular culture.
Another book using rhetoric to deal with

Aristotle

popular culture is Deanna D. Solow's *The Rhetorical Power of
Popular Culture,* published in 2010. In *Messages,* I deal with
many of the topics these rhetoricians write about, such as vari-
eties of rhetorical criticism (Marxist, psychoanalytic, semiotic)
in my chapter (Chapter 3) on rhetorical methods of analyzing
texts plus ways of making sense of images, and I also interpret
important popular culture texts, such as the James Bond novels
and films.

Aristotle, one of the most famous Greek philosophers
(384–322 BCE), transformed our thinking about every topic he
dealt with, and since he wrote about many topics, from politics to ethics, he has been incredibly influential over the years.
His book, *Rhetoric,* was an extremely important study of the
subject and provides us with a useful perspective on the matter. For Aristotle, rhetoric had two components: public speaking and logical discussion. He wrote that while every area of
thought might have its own means of persuasion, only rhetoric
involved persuasion in all fields. As he explained (quoted in
McKeon 1941:1329):

> Rhetoric may be defined as the faculty of observing in any
> given case the available means of persuasion. This is not a
> function of any other art. Every other art can instruct or per-
> suade about its own particular subject-matter; for instance,
> medicine about what is healthy and unhealthy, geometry

about the properties of magnitudes, arithmetic about numbers, and the same is true of the other arts and sciences. But rhetoric we look upon as the **power** of observing the means of persuasion on almost any subject presented to us; and that is why we say that, in its technical character, it is not concerned with any special or definite class of subjects.

He suggested that there are three means of persuasion, which create the elements of a rudimentary communication model:

Ethos, which is based on the personal character and credibility of the speaker.

For example, a general speaks about conflicts and wars.

Pathos, which is based on affecting the emotions of the members of an **audience**.

For example, a politician gives a stirring speech on some subject of importance.

Logos, which is based on the arguments made and logic used by the speaker.

For example, a lawyer defends someone in court.

Aristotle's writings on rhetoric help us understand communication, in general, since much of it is involved in convincing the people we are communicating with about the correctness of our views, in everything from personal conversations to advertisements carried by the mass media. The problem with Aristotle's model is that it suggests that persuasion is the most important element in communication, which is an over-simplification. We do other things when we communicate, such as imparting information, acknowledging someone's presence, and looking for help in solving some problem.

Used in the broadest sense, rhetoric helps us understand why people speak and write the way they do and how they achieve their desired effects. For the Greeks, rhetoric was important because it helped them shape their **values** and come to conclusions about them, and thus live together peacefully. As I suggested earlier, rhetoricians do not always confine themselves to speech but also write about film, political campaigns, popular culture, and other areas where language is used.

The Jakobson Model

We can move beyond an understanding of rhetoric as dealing with persuasion and argumentation and look at the process of communication in general. One of the most important and influential models of communication comes from Roman Jakobson, a Russian linguist who lived from 1896 to 1982. He taught, at the end of his career, at Harvard University and then the Massachusetts Institute of Technology.

Roman Jakobson

Jakobson's model deals with six elements in communication. They are:

Context

Message

Sender------------------------------------**Receiver**

Contact (Medium)

Code

In Jakobson's model, a sender sends a message (some kind of information) to a receiver. The message is transmitted by a code (such as the English language) using a contact (or **medium**, such as speech). The context in which a message is sent also plays an important role in helping the receiver make sense of the message. Thus, the message "pass the hypodermic needle" means one thing in a dark alley and another thing in a hospital.

A concrete explanation of Jakobson's theory can be found in Marcel Danesi's *Understanding Media Semiotics*. Danesi is a semiotician who teaches at the University of Toronto in Canada and has written extensively on popular culture. He uses Superman to deal with the various elements in Jakobson's model (2002:44–45):

The *addresser* is the creator of a particular Superman episode.

The *message* is what a specific episode is designed to convey.

The *addressee* is the audience, i. e. the intended receiver of the Superman episode.

The *context* is what permits an audience to recognize that the episode is authentic....

The mode of *contact* is the method by which the addresser and addressee are linked. In media terms, it is equivalent to the "medium." A Superman episode can be delivered in comic book, TV, radio or movie form.

The *code,* as we saw above, is the system of recurrent story elements that allow audiences to decipher a Superman episode as an adventure story extolling heroism.

Messages, in Jakobson's model, have a number of functions. The most common is the **referential function**, which relates to the surroundings in which speakers find themselves. There are other functions, such as **emotive functions**, which involve the sender expressing feelings, and **poetic functions**, which involve using literary devices, such as metaphors, similes, and word choice, that give a message its tone and distinctive qualities (known as "voice"). We can see these functions in the chart below:

Referential Function	Emotive Function	Poetic Function
It is cold outside.	"To be or not to be?"	"A time to live and a time to die."

Because models are simplifications of complex human phenomena, they don't always fully express the real phenomenon. Jakobson's model, like all models, has these problems. For example, we don't know whether his use of the term "message" deals with the words that are uttered or with the meaning of the words that are uttered. Nevertheless, the model is useful in that it offers us a good overview of the communication process.

The Toulmin Model

Stephen Toulmin was also interested in persuasion, and his model offers a series of steps to be taken to convince others of the soundness of one's position on whatever subject is under consideration. Toulmin, a British philosopher (1929–2009), refined Aristotle's writings on rhetoric. He suggested that good arguments usually have six parts. I list the basic elements in his models below, in my own words:

1. *A* claim *is made about some matter.*
2. *The* grounds *or evidence to support the claim are offered.*
3. *A* warrant, *which is a chain of reasoning that links the ground to the claim, is made.*
4. Backing *is offered to support the warrant.*
5. *A* rebuttal/reservation *is made that rebuts counter arguments or counter claims.*
6. Qualifications and conditionalitys *are offered showing the limits of the claim, warrant, and backing.*

Toulmin's theory is important because he lays out the most important elements in making an argument. First, we must assert something is true or that an argument is correct. Second, we must offer evidence to support our claim. This evidence must be something that reasonable people will accept as valid. Then we must explain the reasoning we use to make our claim, what he calls the "warrant," and also offer evidence or support for the warrant. It is also a good idea, he suggests, to consider arguments against a claim and rebut them. Finally, it makes sense to qualify our assertions and offer conditions under which the claim can be supported.

The logic people use to persuade others is a complicated matter and one that has attracted many different explanations. We can say that, broadly speaking, Aristotle and Toulmin have considerably different approaches to logic, argumentation, and persuasion. Aristotle's model is based on the character of speakers, the emotions they stir in their audiences, and the logic they use, and we can use his model to understand much communication, especially persuasive communication like advertisements. But the model doesn't deal with non-persuasive communication, with qualifying statements in reasoning, the rules of evidence, and the counter claims—what Toulmin calls the "warrant."

The Lasswell Formula

Harold D. Lasswell's model is one of the shortest in communication, but also one of the broadest and most famous. Lasswell (1902–1978) was a political scientist who taught at the University of Chicago and Yale University and offered one of the most well-known and succinct models of the communication process. In 1948, he wrote what has been described as "perhaps the most famous single phrase in communication research" (McQuail and Windahl 1993:13), what is now known as the "Lasswell Formula":

> One convenient way to describe an act of communication is to answer the following questions:
>
> Who?
>
> Says what?
>
> In which channel?
>
> To whom?
>
> With what effect?

This **formula** asks "who" is sending the message, "what" is the message, which channel (means) is being used to deliver the message, "to whom" is it being sent, and what "effect" is it having on the receiver of the message.

Denis McQuail and Sven Windahl, in their book, *Communication Models for the Study of Mass Communication*, point out that the last phrase in Lasswell's model is problematic. They write:

> The Lasswell Formula shows a typical trait of early communication models: it more or less takes for granted that the communicator has some intention of influencing the receiver and, hence, that communication should be treated mainly as a persuasive process. It is also assumed that messages always have effects. Models such as this have contributed to the tendency to exaggerate the effects of, especially, mass communication. (1993:14)

They add that like many other communications theorists, Lasswell's model is uni-directional, going from someone who says something to someone who receives a message and is affected by it. It didn't consider the matter of feedback from those who receive the communication.

Their critique makes two important points: first, by focusing on effects, the Lasswell Formula assumes (like Aristotle) that the purpose of communication is essentially persuasive, and second, it doesn't include responses to communication. It is, then, one-directional—going from who is speaking to an audience and not accounting for feedback from the audiences of communication.

The Focal Points Model

Let me move, now, to a model I developed that deals with the mass media, and the different **focal points** that might be investigated relative to **artists** and creative people, the texts they create, the media they employ, the audiences they seek, and the societies in which they are found. It is also possible to use the model for other kinds of communication, such as **interpersonal communication**, if we leave out the mass media as a focal point.

In my model of communication, found in my book, *Media and Communication Research Methods,* 5th edition (2014), I suggest that there are five focal points that we must consider when dealing with the communication process:

Artist (or group of artists), who "speaks" and creates texts

Art, which is what is said or created; the text

Medium, which carries the text

Audience members, who receive the text

America, which is the society in which a text is created and transmitted

What complicates matters is that every focal point is connected, directly or indirectly, to every other focal point, as we see in this diagram:

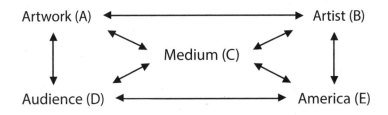

If we are dealing with a conversation, the art work or text becomes what is said by someone, the artist, and the medium is speech. The person who receives the message is the audience, and the process takes place in some group in society, and in a country such as America. The audience in my model can range from one individual to a small group to a huge number of people, which is the case with the mass media.

When dealing with communication, which can range from a conversation to a mass mediated text carried by television or film or radio, we can consider the relationship that exists between artists and the art work, between artists, the art work and America (or society), between the medium and the art work and the audience, and so on, ad infinitum. All of these focal points play a role in the communication process, and researchers have to decide which combination of focal points to consider; in some cases, an analysis can involve all of the focal points. I list some of the simplest relationship possibilities here:

AB artwork and artist

AC artwork and medium

AD artwork and audience

AE artwork and America (or any society)

BC artist and medium

BD artist and audience

BE artist and America (or any society)

CD medium and audience

CE medium and America (or any society)

DE audience and America (or any society)

We can move from dealing with two focal points to more complicated discussions involving three, four, or all five focal points, depending upon our interests.

When I developed my focal points model, I didn't realize its close relationship to the Jakobson and Lasswell models. We can see the relationships in the chart that follows:

Lasswell	Berger	Jakobson
Who?	Artist	Sender
Says what?	Art (text)	Message
In which channel?	Medium	Contact
To whom?	Audience	Receiver
With what effect?	Society (impact on)	Context?

All three models, in varying ways, cover the same things and can be used to analyze most kinds of communication—that is, everything from a personal conversation to a lecture, a television show, or a film. What my model does is show the way different aspects of the communication process are related to one another, whether we are dealing with a conversation between two people or with the mass media. What we learn from this chart is that there are a relatively limited number of elements in the communication process. What this chart does not deal with is the levels in communication—my next subject.

Levels of Communication

There are a number of different levels of communication, such as intrapersonal, interpersonal, small group, and **mass communication**. When we think about communication, it makes sense to keep in mind the level involved, though the theories described in this book often can be used at many levels of communication. Later chapters in this book will deal with each of these levels in more detail.

Intrapersonal Communication

This is the term we use for internal dialogues that often take place in our minds as, so to speak, we talk to ourselves. In this communication, we carry on dialogues with ourselves about some matter that concerns us. Sometimes we even conduct imaginary conversations with others. In other words, we have thoughts about something and spend time talking to ourselves about it. This kind of communication generally takes place in the form of thoughts in our brains, though writing journals and diaries

DICTIONARY of ADVERTISING CONCEPTS

can also be seen as a kind of **intrapersonal communication**. I have written more than ninety journals over the years, and most of my books—including this one—come from material I wrote in my journals. In journals we write to ourselves, which can be thought of as a form of talking to ourselves.

Interpersonal Communication (see Chapter 5)

For our purposes, we will use the term "interpersonal" for communication that takes place between an individual and another individual. Generally, the communicators are acquainted, as in a dinner party, but it can take place between strangers, as, for example, when one gets into a conversation with someone in a supermarket. The medium is generally the human voice (along with body language and facial expressions), though now, in the internet age, it can be text messages to friends or email messages or tweets to a small group of people. The development of smartphones has led to changes in the way we conduct interpersonal communication, with **texting** replacing voice communication much of the time. Texting adds a new dimension to interpersonal communication. There is an element of **alienation** connected to texting—sometimes we text because we want to send a message but don't want to get involved in a conversation.

In our conversations with others, the tone of voice, the strength and nature of a touch (a caress or a firm grasp of someone's arm), the kind of facial expressions and body language we use…all of these things suggest that any given kind of communication can be used to send different messages. I deal with these matters in my chapter on visual communication (Chapter 9).

Small Group Communication (see Chapter 6)

For our purposes, we will consider a small group to be a larger number of people than we find in interpersonal communication —that is, at least three people. Thus, a typical seminar in a university could be considered a small group, but the term also applies to families, clubs and other groupings of people that are relatively small. We can extend the term to cover courses in large lecture halls with hundreds of students or lectures before large audiences. We use the term "small group" to distinguish this level from mass communication, which can cover hundreds of thousands or millions of people. The medium is usually the spoken word, augmented by sound and images, as, for example, when PowerPoint and videos are used.

Mass Communication (see Chapter 7)

This kind of communication involves the use of print, electronic media, videos, and films to reach large numbers of people, who are located in many different places and, in some cases, such as Super Bowl broadcasts, all over the world. In mass communications, a sender or a small group of senders, such as the actors and performers, artists, and technicians involved in making television shows and films, transmit their messages, via print, television, video, audio, film, or the internet to large numbers of receivers—that is, audiences. The members of these audiences may be lone individuals or groups of people of varying sizes. In the United States, a small number of corporations own and control the mass media, but the development of the internet and social media now allow individuals and groups of people to reach large audiences.

One problem with mass communication is that people often interpret messages incorrectly. The Italian semiotician Umberto Eco argues that in mass communications we often have **aberrant decoding** because people from different backgrounds, **socio-economic classes**, and educational levels interpret messages different ways. As he writes in his article, "Towards a Semiotic Inquiry into the Television Message" (1972:15),

> Codes and subcodes are applied to the message in the light of a general framework of cultural references, which constitute the receiver's patrimony of knowledge: his ideological, ethical, religious standpoints, his psychological attitudes, his tastes, his value systems, etc.

We can understand why people do not always interpret messages the way the sender of the messages expects them to be interpreted. For example, script writers may use words people don't understand or make allusions to texts that the members of the audience do not know. If a scriptwriter has a character say that something is "postmodern" and viewers of the show don't know what postmodern means, these viewers won't be able to understand what is going on in the story. Although Eco focused on the mass media, his point can be applied to other kinds of communication. People often make errors in interpreting things said in conversations, as well. Communication, we see, is a process fraught with dangers.

Summary

We see that communication is a complex matter. Many scholars have defined communication, and though there are differences between the definitions, there is a general theme in them which is that communication involves sending messages of one kind or another to others and receiving messages from others. Communication scholars have also created many models of the communication process, one more complicated than the other. There is some question about the matter of effects, for focusing on effects, as Lasswell does, suggests that the basic function of communication is persuasion. Aristotle would agree with Lasswell, but other scholars think such definitions are too limiting. In addition, communication takes place at different levels, from internal thoughts we have about various matters to mass communication, in which there can be audiences of millions of people.

Applications

1. What arguments do scholars make who suggest that communication is central to being human?

2. After studying the models of communication discussed in this chapter, create your own model of the communication process. Will you concern yourself with effects? Explain why or why not.

3. Use the Berger Focal Points model to analyze a film or television show with a focus on the relation between the text, the medium, and the audience.

4. How do Aristotle's and Toulmin's models of rhetoric differ? Give an example to show this.

Chapter 2

Language and Texts

21 consonants

9 vowels

3 semivowels (y, w, r)

4 stresses

4 pitches

1 juncture (pause between words)

3 terminal contours (to end sentences)

TO BE...

Or not.

Words
Dialogism
Codes
Sapir-Whorf
Language Codes
Basil Bernstein

Messages: An Introduction to Communication by Arthur Asa Berger, 34–47.
© 2014 Left Coast Press, Inc. All rights reserved.

The basis of modern media effectiveness is a language within a language—one that communicates to each of us at a level beneath our conscious awareness, one that reaches into the uncharted mechanism of the human unconscious. This is a language based upon the human ability to *subliminally* or *subconsciously* or *unconsciously* perceive information. This is a language that today has actually produced the profit base for North American mass communication media. It is virtually impossible to pick up a newspaper or magazine, turn on a radio or television set, read a promotional pamphlet or the telephone book, or shop through a supermarket without having your subconscious purposely massaged by some monstrously clever artist, photographer, writer, or technician.

Wilson Bryan Key, *Subliminal Seduction*

Linguists and philosophers have long been saying that language limits the possibilities of thought. But language is not an independent variable, nor is thought controlled and formed by it. For both speech and thought are dependent parts of human communication. The control is not in the speech form but in the set of human relations which generate thought and speech. Basil Bernstein has focused upon this angle of the ancient problem. He asks what are the main kinds of social relations—what structuring in society itself calls for its own appropriate structures of speech.

Mary Douglas, *Implicit Meanings*

The building blocks of verbal communication are words, combined to create texts, and understood within a context of understanding known as language. This language, as the Key quotation suggests, may affect us in ways that we do not recognize and is an important theme in this book. I begin with Peter Farb's discussion of the importance of words and Mikhail Bakhtin's analysis of what happens when we put words together into speech in our conversations. Then I turn to Catherine Riessman's discussion of codes in conversation, the Sapir-Whorf **hypothesis**, and Basil Bernstein's research on language codes.

Peter Farb on Words

Farb explains in *Word Play: What Happens When People Talk*
that we always are following rules when we speak in the same
the way people do when they play games. Learning a language
involves learning how to follow a number of complicated rules
that we acquire unconsciously as we grow up. We internalize
the rules to which we've been exposed. We may not be aware
of all these rules, but the fact that we are guided by them is
demonstrated when we recognize when someone has not used
the rules correctly. Thus, parents frequently have to tell to their
children how to speak correctly. If a child says, "I seen Jim at
the playground," the parents says, "Not seen but saw. I saw Jim
at the playground." As Farb explains (1974:7):

> Unless he is a specialist in the subject of language, he most
> likely is unaware that he is following various complicated
> sets of rules which he has unconsciously acquired and inter-
> nalized. Yet it is clear that he has incorporated such rules,
> for he recognizes speech that is "wrong"—that is, speech
> that departs from the rules—even though he does not con-
> sciously know the rules themselves.

Farb's discussion of the rules of language that we obey has
implications for other areas of communication. His writings
suggest that there are certain codes that we learn which shape
not only our use of language, but other areas of our lives as well.

Words are made up of **phonemes**, a Greek term (which literally means "sound unit") for the smallest significant unit
of *sound*. According to *The Random House Dictionary of the
English Language*, phonemes are "the basic units of sounds by
which **morphemes**, words and sentences are represented."

The English language has several hundred thousand words,
which are all created, Farb writes, out of just three dozen
sounds—and they are selected from the many different sounds
of which the human voice is capable. As Farb explains:

Linguists...generally agree that the language game is played with the following 45 phoneme "pieces":

21 consonants

9 vowels

3 semivowels (y, w, r)

4 stresses

4 pitches

1 juncture (pause between words)

3 terminal contours (to end sentences)

These 45 phonemes used in English today represent the total sound resources by which speakers can create an infinity of utterances. (1974:6–14, 294)

Our languages enable us to speak to one another—using words—and convey information, feelings, and all kinds of other things. Farb writes that we learn our languages when we are young children. By around one year of age, children generally can speak recognizable words. Once children master language, they can speak sentences they've never heard or seen. Language, then, becomes the cornerstone of culture, and it is words and the "rules" that tell us how to use them to shape, in varying degrees, our sense of ourselves and our place in society.

Farb turns his attention to the codes and rules that shape language and the importance of the culture, **subculture**, or what he calls "speech community," in shaping our language use. He writes:

You've already said this.... Language is both a system of grammar and a human behavior which can be analyzed according to theories of interaction, play, and games. It can also be viewed as a shared system of rules and conventions, mutually intelligible to all members of a particular community, yet a system which nevertheless offers freedom and creativity in its use.... For the rest of his life the child will speak sentences he has never before heard, and when he thinks or reads, he will still literally talk to himself. He can never escape from speech. And from speech flow all the other hallmarks of our humanity: those arts, sciences, laws, morals, customs, political and economic systems, and religious faiths that collectively are known as "culture."

A language is like a game played with a fixed number of pieces—phonemes—each one easily recognized by native speakers. This is true of every language, except that the pieces change from one language game to another. (1974:6–14, 294)

It is words, then, that shape our consciousness, our communication, and our culture. "What is honor?" Shakespeare's Falstaff asks. He answers, "A word. What is that word honor? What is that honor? Air." For Falstaff, a word is mere air. For linguists, words are not air but everything—the building blocks of language and culture.

Mikhail Bakhtin on Dialogism

Mikhail Bakhtin (1895–1975), a Russian scholar, developed a theory called "**dialogism**" that argued that all conversations are based on two considerations—what was said before and what will be said in the future. As he explains in his book, *The Dialogic Imagination: Four Essays* (1981: 280):

Mikhail
Bakhtin

> The word in living conversation is directly, blatantly, oriented toward a future answer-word: it provokes an answer, anticipates it and structures itself on the answer's direction. Forming itself in an atmosphere of the already spoken, the word is at the same time determined by that which has not yet been said but which is needed and in fact anticipated by the answering word. Such is the situation in any living dialogue.

So speech becomes complicated by the fact that when we converse, we build upon speech from the past (generally this process is **unconscious**), and, at the same time, we help shape speech in the future. If we apply this notion to mass mediated texts, such as television programs and films, we can gain some insight into what is known as **intertextuality**, which suggests that all texts are related, in complicated ways, to earlier texts.

When we have a conversation with someone, we recall what was said earlier and anticipate what might be said later in the conversation, either by ourselves or by the person(s) with whom we are speaking.

According to Bakhtin, all texts—this is the term we use in scholarly discourse for all works such as films, paintings, novels, advertisements, commercials, comic strips, letters, emails, text messages, and so on—quote, either consciously or unconsciously, from works from the past. Describing writings in the Middle Ages, he explains (1981:69):

> One of the best authorities on medieval parody…states outright that the history of medieval literature and its Latin literature in particular "is the history of appropriation, re-working and imitation of someone else's property"—or as we would say, of another's language, another's style, another's word.

What happened in the Middle Ages, the "appropriation" of the work of others, is common today. This is because many people in the Western world share a common cultural heritage which shapes the work of artists and writers (and all creative people) and is reflected in texts even when the creators of these texts didn't make a conscious decision made to "quote" from other texts or sources.

Many texts consciously "quote" from—that is, are based upon—earlier texts, such as the Bible or Shakespeare or Greek mythology or important novels, plays, and films. Thus, the musical play, *West Side Story*, was based on Shakespeare's *Romeo and Juliet*, and James Joyce's novel *Ulysses* was based on Homer's *The Odyssey*. The film *The Avengers* (2012) is based on various Marvel comics heroes and other superhero films.

These examples of intertextuality are easy to see and were done consciously. What Bakhtin argues is that, as in conversations, where our speech is based on past speech and our anticipation of future

William Shakespeare

speech, all works of art are, by necessity, intertextual and borrow from other works, even though the creators of the new works of art are not always consciously doing so. Sometimes this borrowing involves plots, sometimes it involves themes, sometimes it involves language, and sometimes it involves images and a style that remind us of earlier texts. In essence, he is arguing that "there's nothing new under the sun," a phrase found in the Bible.

Codes in Conversations

William Labov and Joshua Waletsky, two linguistics scholars whose writings (1960s–1980s) are often technical and difficult and whose ideas are scattered in long articles and books, contend that every conversation has the following elements in it. Here is my list of their elements, as based on Riessman:

An abstract that gives an overview and summary of things

An orientation that provides us with the who, what, where, when, and why

A complicating action that tells the sequence of events that transpired

An evaluation that deals with the importance and meaning of events recounted

A resolution that tells us how the story ended

A coda that returns the recitation of the story to the present time

These elements are necessary for us to tell stories and answer any questions our listeners might have about the conversation or story. Sociologist Catherine Kohler Riessman explains of Labov/Waletzsky's work:

> In *Poetics*, Aristotle said that a narrative has a beginning, middle, and end. Ever since, scholars agree that sequence is necessary, if not sufficient, for narrative.... Labov and Waletzksy (1967) argued that stories follow a chronicle sequence. The order of events moves in a linear way through time and the "order cannot be changed without changing the inferred sequence of events in the original semantic

interpretation." A narrative, according to this definition, is always responding to the question "and then what happened?"... In conversation, tellers sometimes let listeners know a story is coming and indicate when it is over, with entrance and exit talk.... "Once upon a time" and "they lived happily ever after" are classic examples in folktales of bracketing devices. But stories told in research interviews are rarely so clearly bounded, and locating them is often a complex interpretive process. Where one chooses to begin and end a narrative can profoundly alter its shape and meaning. (Riessman 1993:17–19)

Like weight bearing walls, personal narratives depend on certain structures to hold them together. Stories told in conversation share common parameters, although they may be put together in contrasting ways and, as a result, point to different interpretations.

Events become meaningful because of their placement in a narrative. As Riessman explains (1993:18):

Labov's...structural approach is paradigmatic.... Narratives, he argues, have formal properties and each has a function.... With these structures, a teller constructs a story from a primary experience and interprets the significance of events in clauses and embedded evaluations.

Of course not every conversation involves telling stories, but many do, and the six elements are generally found in conversations, because they satisfy needs listeners have to understand what is being recounted.

The Sapir-Whorf Hypothesis

Bakhtin emphasized the importance of language in conversation and in the arts, and Labov and Waletzsky dealt with the codes found in most conversations. The **Sapir-Whorf Hypothesis** also deals with language and the way the words we use in our messages shape, in part, the responses people give to our messages, as well as people's perceptions of society and the world. Edward Sapir (1884–1939) was an anthropologist who did research on language, and Benjamin Whorf (1897–1941) was his student. What is known as the Sapir-Whorf Hypothesis combines ideas both had. As Sapir explains in his essay, "Language and Experience" (1931:78):

> The relation between language and experience is often misunderstood. Language is not a more or less systematic inventory of the various items of experience which seem relevant to the individual, as is so often naively assumed, but is also a self-contained, creative symbolic organization, which not only refers to experience largely acquired without its help but actually defines experience for us by reason of its formal completeness and because of our unconscious projection of its implicit expectations into the field of experience.... Such categories as number, gender, case, tense, mode, voice, "aspect" and a host of others, many of which are not recognized...are, of course derivative of experience at last analysis, but, once abstracted from experience, they are systematically elaborated in language and are not so much discovered in experience as imposed upon it because of the tyrannical hold that linguistic form has upon our orientation in the world.

For Sapir and Whorf, language plays a dominant role in shaping our perceptions of the world and can be seen as a kind of prism that we use to make sense of the world. The language we learn as we grow up in a particular family in a specific socio-economic **class** in society in a particular country affects us in profound ways.

Think, for example, of the difference between Bostonian accents and southern accents or the many different accents in England. What we know of society and the world is tied to the language habits of the family, group, class, or sub-culture in which we find ourselves. As Sapir wrote in *Language*, "The worlds in which different societies live are distinct worlds, not merely the same world with different labels attached" (quoted in DeFleur and Ball-Rokeach 1982:138). Language becomes, then, a central factor in the way we live and think about the world.

Basil Bernstein

Basil Bernstein on Language Codes

A British socio-linguist, Basil Bernstein (1924–2000), did some research on the way different socio-economic classes in Britain used language and concluded that children there, depending upon their class, learned different language codes by which they understood the world and their place in it. These codes are the "elaborated" code and the "restricted" code, and the codes children learn shape their future development and adult life. He discusses these codes in his article, "Social Class, Language and Socialization" (in Giglioli 1972: 164).

I shall argue that forms of socialization orient the child towards speech codes which control access to relatively context-tied or relatively context-independent meanings. Thus I shall argue that elaborated codes orient their users towards universalistic meanings, whereas **restricted codes** orient, sensitize, their users to particularistic meanings: that the linguistic-realization of the two orders are different, and so are the social relationships which realize them. Elaborated codes are less tied to a given or local structure and thus contain the potentiality of change in principles.

In the case of elaborated codes the speech is freed from its evoking social structure and *takes* on an autonomy. A university is a place organized around talk. Restricted codes are more tied to a local social structure and have a reduced potential for disuse in principles. Where codes are elaborated, the socialized has more access to the grounds of his own socialization, and so can enter into a reflexive relationship to the social order he has taken over. Where codes are restricted, the socialized has less access to the grounds of his socialization, and thus reflexiveness may be limited in range. One of the effects of the class system is to limit access to elaborated codes.

I shall go on to suggest that restricted codes…draw upon metaphor whereas elaborated codes draw upon rationality. That these codes constrain the contextual use of language in critical socializing contexts and in this way regulate the orders of relevance and relations which the socialized takes over. From this point of view, change in habitual speech codes involves changes in the means by which object and person relationships are realized.

The differences between these codes are shown here in a chart I made based on Bernstein's ideas:

Elaborated Code	Restricted Code
Middle classes and above	Working classes
Grammatically complex language	Grammatically simple language
Varied vocabulary	Uniform vocabulary
Complex sentence structure	Short, repetitive sentence structure
With what effect?	Society (impact on)
Careful use of adjective and adverbs	Little use of adjectives and adverbs
High level of conceptualization	Low level of conceptualization
Logical	Emotional
Use of qualifications	Little use of qualifications
Users aware of code	Users unaware of code

Let me offer examples:

Restricted code: "Get something for the dog!"

Elaborated code: "When you're in town, please stop off in the pet store and get a chew toy for Rover."

The language that children use becomes a matrix through which they see the world and through which their thoughts are processed. If Bernstein is correct, the codes that children in the different classes learn explains why there are such differences between working class and middle and upper class British

people in their values, their **lifestyles**, and, most particularly, their occupations.

In her book, *Implicit Meanings,* the English social anthropologist Mary Douglas (1921–2007) discusses the work of Basil Bernstein in a chapter titled "Humans Speak." What Bernstein did, she suggests, is force us to recognize that speech is connected to the socio-economic classes and social relations in which speakers find themselves and that, as Douglas puts it, "The distribution of speech forms is equally a realization of the distribution of power" (1975:177). How we speak, then, is connected to how we were brought up and the socio-economic class into which we were born.

Summary

In this chapter, I dealt with Peter Farb's ideas about words and language, Mikhail Bakhtin's notion of intertextuality and the way texts are related to one another, and the codes that shape our conversations. I also explained the Sapir-Whorf Hypothesis, which suggests that language shapes our perceptions and Basil Bernstein's work on restricted and elaborated codes and their impact on people's lives. Language, we learn, not only tells us who we are but also helps determine who we will be.

Applications

1. Make an intertextual analysis of a text. Take a film or television program and show how it "borrows" themes, plots, and characters or has been affected by other films or television programs.

2. What do researchers say about creativity? How do you define it? Is everyone creative? Explain your answer.

3. How do Bakhtin's theories relate to creativity in the arts? Explain your answer.

4. Analyze a conversation between characters in a television show and see the extent to which you can apply the conversational codes discussed in this chapter.

5. What do contemporary linguists say about the Sapir-Whorf hypothesis? Is it considered valid? What criticisms do they have of it?

Chapter 3

Rhetorical Methods for Analyzing Texts

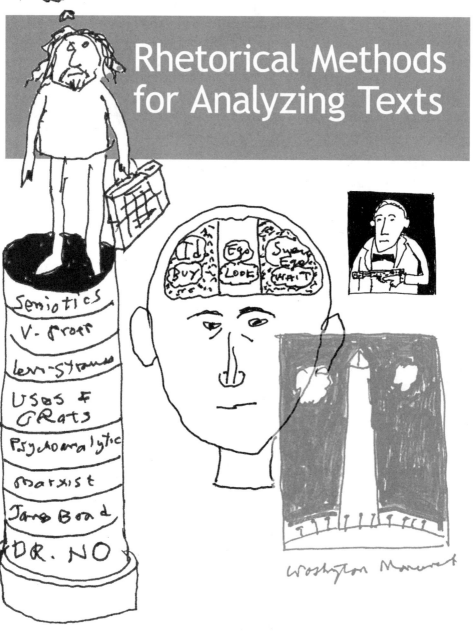

Messages: An Introduction to Communication by Arthur Asa Berger, 48–87.

During all these centuries in which rhetoric was defined primarily in terms of traditional texts, people still experienced signs, artifacts, and texts that were not in that traditional form. Informal conversation, architecture, clothing styles, common entertainments, food—in short a whole range of cultural artifacts other than traditional rhetorical texts—were experienced by people as influential and moving, while rhetorical theorists continued to call only the traditional texts rhetoric.

Barry Brummett, *Rhetoric in Popular Culture*, 3rd Edition

The supreme virtue of psychoanalysis, from the point of view of its potential utility for literary study, is that it has investigated the very aspects of man's nature with which the greatest writers of fiction have been preoccupied: the emotional unconscious or only partly comprehended bases of our behavior. Unlike other psychologies, but like Sophocles and Shakespeare, Tolstoy and Dostoevsky, Melville and Hawthorne, it has concerned itself with the surging non-rational forces which play so large a part in determining our destiny as well as the part of our being which tries, often in vain, to control and direct them. It offers a systematic and well-validated body of knowledge about those forces.

It ought to be apparent that the finding of such a psychology should be helpful in explicating many of the things conveyed through fiction—and in particular the deepest levels of meaning of the greatest fiction. I deliberately use the word *explicate*. It is my assumption that as we read we unconsciously *understand* at least some of a story's secret significance; to some extent our enjoyment is a product of this understanding. But some readers go on to try to account for the effect a story has had upon them, and to report what they discover. It is in connection with these later critical activities, which must be differentiated I believe from the reading experience itself, that psychoanalytic concepts are likely to prove invaluable. They make it possible to deal with a portion of our response which was not hitherto accessible to criticism—permit us to explain reactions which were intuitive, fugitive and often non-verbal, and supply the key to the elements in the story responsible for those reactions.

Simon Lesser, *Fiction and the Unconscious*

When we say we are going to watch some television, what we really mean is that we are going to watch some program or kind of program that interests us—"Sixty Minutes," a baseball game, a football game, a mystery, a politic procedural, a news show, a talk show, and so on. In this chapter I will discuss methods of textual analysis—the disciplines and theories we use to analyze and interpret texts in order to understand how we find meaning in them and what their semiotic, psychoanalytic, sociological, and political significance may be. I also discuss **genres**—the kinds of shows and films we watch. I should point out that the texts we analyze are the sites for battles between critics with different perspectives on things who apply different methodologies to texts. This chapter shows, as Brummett explains in the epigraph, that rhetorical analysis has moved far beyond the traditional subject of rhetorical analysis—speech.

In this chapter, we will cover four well-known models of understanding and analyzing texts. I begin with semiotics (originally known as semiology), the science of signs and the ideas of Ferdinand de Saussure (1857–1913), author of a seminal book on the subject, *Course in General Linguistics*, and the other founding father of semiotics, American philosopher Charles Sanders Peirce (1839–1914). I will also offer material on sociological theory (and its focus on the uses people make of texts and the gratifications that texts offer people), Marxist theory, and Freud's contributions to psychoanalytic theory. To demonstrate these analytic strategies, I will use the James Bond spy story **Dr. No**, written by Ian Fleming.

Semiotic Analysis

There are, it turns out, more than 11,000 books on semiotics listed on Amazon.com and more than one million sites (as of July 21, 2014) in a Google search on the subject. So though many people aren't familiar with the term, "semiotics" isn't as obscure as we might imagine. In an article about semiotics, "How They Know What You Really Mean" (1982), Maya Pines offers us an important insight into what semiotics is all about. She explains that everything we do sends messages to others and others are always sending messages about themselves to us—in various codes. These messages are found in such things as the foods we eat, the music we like, our **gestures**, our facial expressions, and our entertainments. Semiotics, Pines suggests, teaches us how to find meaning in all the objects and other kinds of messages that others send to us and how others find meaning in the messages we send to them. I begin this examination of semiotics and the way it helps us find meaning in the world with the Swiss linguist Ferdinand de Saussure.

Ferdinand de Saussure and Semiology

Ferdinand de Saussure

Ferdinand de Saussure, one of the founding fathers of semiotics, the science of signs, had important insights to offer us about language. In his book, *Course in General Linguistics,* published in 1915, he made a distinction between *language,* which is a human institution, human *speech,* and what individuals say when they speak, which he called *parole.* As he wrote, "But what is language [*langue*]? It is not to be confused with human speech [*langage*], of which it is only a definite part, though certainly an essential one" (1915/1966:9). A few pages later, on page 13, he adds, "Execution is always individual, and the individual is always its master: I shall call the executive side *speaking* [*parole*]." Thus, we have three levels of language. I explain how they differ by using fashion as an example.

Langue	Langage	Parole
Language	Speech	Speaking
Social Institution	Individual/Social	Individual action
Fashion	Clothes in a wardrobe	What a person wears

Fashion is a good topic to show the relationship between langue, langage, and parole. Notice in the following ad that we only see part of a woman, her legs, which enables the advertiser to focus on her bag, a bracelet she is wearing, and her shoes.

Fashion ad
for handbag.

Fashion, which we can understand to be all the clothes available, is a social institution, the langue, and like all social institutions, has an effect on individuals. Langage here represents all the clothes a person owns—what the individual has selected from the institution of fashion. And parole represents what a person is wearing at a given point in time, which has been selected from that person's wardrobe. In the realm of speech, langue would be all the words in a language, langage would be all the words in a person's vocabulary, and speech would be what that person says at any moment in time.

Saussure focused attention on signs, which is the basic concept in what he called semiology and what we now call semiotics. Semiotics is the science of signs. The Greek word *sēmeîon* means "sign." Saussure divided signs into two components: every sign, he explained, is made of sound-images, or what he called *signifiers*, and the concepts generated by the signifiers, what he called *signifieds*. What complicates matters is that for Saussure the relation between signifiers and signifieds is arbitrary and based on convention. We call a woody perennial plant with a single large stem and no branches on its lower parts a tree, but we could easily have called it something else. That means we have to learn what the signifieds mean and have to recognize that their meanings can change. Thus, long hair in men used to signify "artistic," but now long hair has lost that meaning; it can mean anything nowadays: poets, truck drivers, and baseball pitchers now often have long hair.

Saussure adds, then, that language is a system of signs and offers what is one of the charter statements of the science of semiology (1915/1966:16):

> Language is a system of signs that express ideas, and is therefore comparable to a system of writing, the alphabet of deaf-mutes, symbolic rites, polite formulas, military signals, etc. But it is the most important of all these systems.
>
> *A science that studies the life of signs within society* is conceivable; it would be a part of social psychology and consequently of general psychology; I shall call it *semiology* (from Greek *sēmeîon* "sign"). Semiology would show what constitutes signs, what laws govern them. Since the science does not yet exist, no one can say what it would be; but it has a right to existence, a place staked out in advance.

Saussure offered another important insight, namely that concepts have meaning because of relations between them, and the basic relationship is oppositional. "In language there are only differences," he wrote (1915/1966: 120), and, he added, "Concepts are purely differential and defined not by their positive content but negatively by their relations with the other terms of the system" (117). Thus, it is not "content" that determines the meaning of a concept, but its "relations" in some kind of a system. The "most precise characteristic" of these concepts "is in being what the others are not" (117). For Saussure, "signs function, then, not through their intrinsic value but through their relative position" (118). We can see this readily enough in language, but it also holds for texts. Nothing has meaning in itself!

C. S. Peirce and Semiotics

C. S. Peirce

C. S. Peirce (1839–1914), an American philosopher, was the second founding father of semiotics. He did an enormous amount of complicated theoretical work on semiotics, but for our purposes—and our interest here is basically in applied semiotics—his trichotomy is of most importance. He wrote that there are three kinds of signs: icons, indexes, and **symbols**. *Icons* signify by resemblance, *indexes* signify by cause and effect, and *symbols* signify on the basis of convention. As he explained:

> Every sign is determined by its objects, either first by partaking in the characters of the object, when I call a sign an *Icon;* secondly, by being really and in its individual existence connected with the individual object, when I call the sign an *Index;* thirdly, by more or less approximate certainty that it will be interpreted as denoting the object, in consequence of a habit (which term I use as including a natural disposition), when I call the sign a *Symbol.* (quoted in Zeman 1977: 36)

Thus, a photograph would be an icon (signifying by resemblance), smoke coming out of a house would be an index (signifying by cause and effect), and flags are symbols (one must learn what flags for different countries look like). The term "iconic" also now has another meaning and is used loosely to refer to people, places, objects, and so on that are noteworthy or of some importance. Thus, an iPhone is an iconic smartphone.

Peirce defined a sign as "something which stands to somebody for something in some respect or capacity" (quoted in Zeman 1977:27) which puts the interpreters of signs in the middle of things and makes them play an important role. He also wrote, "This universe is perfused with signs, if it is not composed exclusively of signs," (quoted in Sebeok 1977:v), which means that semiotics becomes the master science. Every other science becomes, in effect, a sub-discipline of semiotics. These statements about signifiers and signifieds from Saussure and about icons, indexes, and symbols from Peirce, provide us with basic concepts that enable us to analyze phenomena, of all kinds, from a semiotic perspective. Saussure and Peirce differed in their notions about symbols, but for our purposes this difference is not important.

Umberto Eco and Lying with Signs

One other interesting thing about signs is that they are often used to lie. Many blondes we see are really brunettes, red heads, and women with black hair who have dyed their hair, and some beautiful women we see turn out to be men who are cross-dressing. A contemporary semiotician, Umberto Eco, explained that signs can be used to lie. As he wrote in *A Theory of Semiotics* (1976:7):

Umberto Eco

> Semiotics is concerned with everything that can be taken as a sign. A sign is everything which can be taken as significantly substituting for something else. This something else does not necessarily have to exist or to actually be somewhere at the moment in which a sign stands for it. Thus semiotics is in principle the discipline studying everything which can be used in order to lie. If something cannot be used to tell a lie, conversely it cannot be used to tell the truth; it cannot be used "to tell" at all. I think that the definition of a "theory of the lie" should be taken as a pretty comprehensive program for a general semiotics.

Eco's cautionary note about signs alerts us to the fact that many people "lie" with signs. In some cases the lies are trivial and inconsequential, but lies can be very consequential. A brunette who dyes her hair blonde is "telling," so to speak, a trivial lie, as is a bald man wearing a wig. But a person who impersonates a physician can do a great deal of harm, as does a double agent, who pretends to be working as a spy for one country but is really working for a different one.

Saussure's statement that "in language there are only differences" is what is behind the search critics often make for bipolar oppositions in texts—rich and poor, happy and sad, and so forth, which allegedly explains their hidden meaning.

As Jonathan Culler wrote in his book, *Saussure* (1976:15), "Structuralists have generally followed Jakobson and taken the binary opposition as a fundamental operation of the human mind basic to the production of meaning." Generally speaking, we find meaning in texts by analyzing them in terms of bipolar oppositions found in them because our minds find meaning in life, in general, in terms of bipolar oppositions.

One problem is that semioticians sometimes come up with different sets of opposition for the same text; it isn't always a simple as one might imagine. Let me offer an example of the way critics can disagree with one another when making paradigmatic analyses of a text. I will deal with Ian Fleming's famous novel about English spy James Bond, *Dr. No.*

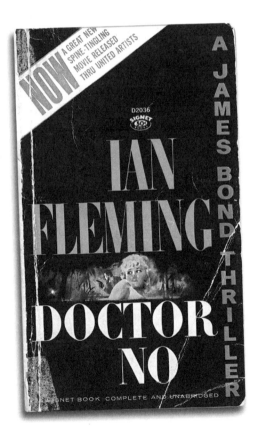

A Synopsis of *Dr. No*

The book begins with two British spies stationed in Jamaica being murdered, in a rather sadistic manner, by some "Chigroes," Chinese Negroes. When the spies don't report to the head office, the spy agency decides to investigate. Chief of the agency, "M," sends Bond to Jamaica to investigate. "It'll be more of a rest cure than anything," M says to a doctor who suggested that Bond should be given more time to rest. M tells Bond he is sending him to Jamaica on what looks like it will be a holiday. Bond is told that the two agents have disappeared and M wants Bond to find out what happened. Bond is briefed about the events in Jamaica and learns about a bird, the Roseate Spoonbill, whose guano was very valuable during the war. He also finds out about the man who owns a small, isolated island where the Spoonbills deposit their guano. "Who is this man?" he asks the chief of staff, who is briefing Bond about the case. The chief of staff replies, "Chinaman, or rather half Chinese and half German. Got a daft name. Calls himself Doctor No—Doctor Julius No!"

Bond then learns about various people who had been killed on the island, supposedly through accidents of one kind or another. "So, in the end the whole fairy story was dumped in our lap," continues the chief.

In a way Bond felt sure he was being sent on this cushy assignment to humiliate him. When Bond flies to Jamaica, there are various attempts to kill him that I will not deal with here. Bond and a helper, Quarrel, steal onto the island one night on a small boat and go to sleep there. In a chapter titled "The Elegant Venus," Bond sees a naked girl, Honeychile Rider, who is collecting sea shells. "She was not a coloured girl," Fleming takes pains to tell us. She had found a bed of valuable Venus Elegans shells. She is described as an exquisite goddess except for one thing—she has an ugly broken nose. Shortly after Bond meets Honeychile, Quarrel is killed and Bond and Honeychile Rider are captured by a Chigro in a truck with a flame thrower, and they are put into a very posh room, which is described as a mink-lined prison. And they are invited to dinner with Dr. No later that night. Fleming describes Dr. No as follows (1958:71):

> Dr. No was at least six inches taller than Bond, but the straight, immovable poise of his body made him seem still taller. The head also was elongated and tapered from a round, completely bald skull down to a sharp chin so that the impression was that of a reversed raindrop—or rather oildrop, for the skin was of a deep almost translucent yellow…. The bizarre, gliding figure looked like a giant venomous worm wrapped in grey tin foil.

Dr. No asks Bond what he would like to drink, and Bond answers, "A medium vodka dry martini—with a slice of lemon peel. Shaken and not stirred, please. I would prefer Russia or Polish vodka." Having his drinks shaken and not stirred is meant to be a signifier of Bond's refined aesthetic sensibilities and is a defining characteristic of Bond. In a chapter titled "Pandora's Box," Bond learns about Dr. No's life. As Bond sizes Dr. No up, he decides that No is "too strong, too well equipped." Dr. No recounts how he is the son of a German Methodist minister and a Chinese girl and was born in Pekin (Beijing). He was rejected by his parents and given to an aunt to bring up. He adds (1958:136), "No love, you see, Mister Bond. Lack of parental care." In Pekin he joined a tong, and, as he explains (1958:136):

> I enjoyed the conspiracies, the burglaries, the arson of insured properties. They represented revolt against the father figure who had betrayed me. I loved the death and destruction of people and things…Then there was trouble. I had to be got out of the way. The Tongs considered me too valuable to kill.

He was smuggled into the United States. As a result of police action, his tong was disrupted, and just before a police raid, Dr. No stole a million dollars and went underground in Harlem. He was found by his tong. They cut off his hands to show he was a thief and shot him through the heart. What they didn't know is that Dr. No's heart was on the right side of his body, so he survived. He used his money to buy expensive stamps so he could transfer his money more easily, and he changed his appearance.

Later he tells Bond that his men have murdered the two missing agents and their bodies are at the bottom of the sea. Dr. No tells Bond and Honeychile that he will be in partnership with Russians to turn the island into a technology center for international espionage. He also has been controlling missiles carrying atomic weapons by interfering with the controlling messages from American bases. He adds that he needs a white woman for a small experiment he has in mind. During the dinner, Bond is able to steal a knife and a cigarette lighter. Dr. No explains that he wants to compare the amount of pain Honeychile can endure with an experiment he conducted previously with a black woman—by staking her on the ground, naked, in the path of black crabs that are migrating and that supposedly devour anything in their path. The black girl died of a heart attack before the crabs got to her.

After dinner, Bond is taken to a concrete cell with nothing in it but Bond's canvas jeans and his blue shirt. The guard tells him he can either sit in his cell and rot or "find your way out on to the course." Bond notices a ventilation grill in a corner of the room, just below the ceiling. He sharpens his knife to a point. Then he tries pulling the grill down and receives an electric shock. He then assumes that he was shocked to help soften him up, and when he tries to remove the grate the second time, there is no shock. He decides to use the wire grate as a kind of spear. Then Bond is subjected to and endures various hazards, such as heat, tarantulas, a fall down a hundred foot shaft into the sea, and a fight with a giant squid. He makes his way to the land, kills a man who is running a crane that is loading guano onto a ship, and unloads the guano on Dr. No, burying him under a mound of guano. He takes a gun from the man he has killed, rescues Honeychile, escapes from the island with her and then, his tasks accomplished, after he pays to have her nose fixed, makes love to her.

A Paradigmatic Analysis of *Dr. No*

Umberto Eco analyzed Ian Fleming's novels and suggests that the basic opposition in them is between Bond and the villains. Thus, the basic opposition in *Dr. No* would be between James Bond and Dr. No, with Honeychile Rider, the heroine, functioning as a mediating figure between them. I suggest there is a different set of oppositions that explains the book and various relationships better. In my analysis of the book I see Dr. No and Honeychile Rider as opposites, with James Bond playing a mediating role. Let me offer the opposition I find in the book:

Honeychile Rider	Bond	Dr. Julius No
Beautiful		Ugly
Natural		Artificial (metal hands)
White		Yellow
Female		Male
Victim		Villain
Lives		Dies
Makes love to Bond		Is killed by Bond

My argument is that these oppositions are the dominant ones in the book: male/female, beautiful/ugly, white/yellow, and so on. It is James Bond who mediates between Honeychile and Dr. No and resolves the opposition by killing No. The question we might ask is—who is right when critics come up with different paradigmatic analyses of texts? I would answer this by suggesting that the critic whose oppositions explain the book better is the correct one. It all depends on how one decides on what are the basic oppositions in the text and justifies one's position.

Sociological Analysis

Sociological analysts of communication look at texts in terms of various sociological concepts that deal with such topics as the age, roles, race, socio-economic status, **gender**, and other similar considerations of characters in dramatic texts. What roles do women generally have in these texts? How are they portrayed? What groups are over-represented and under-represented in them? How are the roles of characters shaped by **stereotypes** people have of African-Americans, women, Latinos, Jews, White Anglo-Saxon Protestants (WASPs), and other groups? What effects do certain texts have on audiences in the United States and on American society at large? And, finally, why do audiences like certain shows and not like others? These questions lead to my discussion of one of the most interesting aspects of media, the audiences of certain kinds of texts and the **uses and gratifications** the texts provide to fans of different genres.

We might consider Fleming's attitudes towards various social, racial, and religious groups in *Dr. No.* The book is a full of racist and anti-Semitic themes. When Bond arrives in Jamaica, the colonial secretary gives Bond a disquisition on the nature of society in Jamaica:

> The Jamaican is a kindly lazy man with the virtues and vices of a child. He lives on a very rich island but he doesn't get rich from it. He doesn't know how to and he's too lazy. The British come and go and take the easy pickings…It's the Portuguese Jews who make the most. They came here with the British and they've stayed. But they're snobs and they spend too much of their fortunes on building fine houses and giving dances…Then come the Syrians, very rich too, but not such good businessmen…Then there are the Indians with their usual flashy trade in soft goods and the like…Finally there are the Chinese, solid, discreet—the most powerful clique in Jamaica. They've got the bakeries and the laundries and the best food stores. They keep to themselves and keep their strain pure…Not that they don't take the black girls when they want them. You can see the result all over Kingston—Chigroes—Chinese negroes and negresses. The Chigroes are

a tough, forgotten race. They look down on Negroes and the Chinese look down on them…They've got some of the intelligence of the Chinese and most of the vices of the black man. (1958:51–52).

Because of all the excitement and curious behaviors found in Bond—his shaken drinks, his sexual exploits with gorgeous women, and his world travel, we don't notice the racism, anti-Semitism, and sexism in most of his novels, but they are quite evident in *Dr. No.*

Sociological Analysis of Uses and Gratifications

We might ask ourselves why genres like spy stories are so popular. Genres make it easy for people to understand what kind of events can be expected in a text and what the events mean, but they also provide a number of psychological gratifications for audiences of generic texts. My focus here is on the psychological payoff that genres provide and on the uses people make of generic texts. Some of the research in the uses and gratifications approach deals with listening to soap operas, reading comic books, and reading romance fiction novels. A number of mass communication scholars are troubled by the uses and gratifications approach because it is very difficult to quantify the uses people make of genres and to tie events in a given text to a particular gratification. Nevertheless, it is quite obvious that people read genre or "pulp" novels, watch soap operas on television, read comic books, and listen to rap or country-western songs because they provide a number of gratifications to their audiences.

A media sociologist, Elihu Katz, and several colleagues wrote an essay, "Utilization of Mass Communication by the Individual" (1979), which explains this perspective in more detail and mentions some work by early researchers in the area (215):

Herzog (1942) on quiz programs and the gratifications derived from listening to soap operas. Suchman (1942) on the motives for getting interested in serious music on radio; Wolfe and Fiske (1949) on the development of children's interest in comics; Berelson (1949) on the functions of newspaper reading; and so on. Each of these investiga-tions came up with a list of functions served either by some specific contents or by the medium in question: to match one's wits against others, to get information or advice for daily living, to provide a framework for one's day, to prepare oneself culturally for the demands of upward mobility, or to be reassured about the dignity and usefulness of one's role.

These studies and others suggest that people use texts for varying purposes and regard these texts as functional for them. They use them to find out how to solve problems they may be experiencing, and the texts provide topics to discuss with friends, enhancing **socialization.** What uses and gratification theorists argue is that members of an audience are not passive but active and selective in choosing certain texts (or genres) that provide various gratifications that they seek.

Here I list a number of the more common and important uses to which people put mass-mediated texts and some of the gratifications they derive from these texts. This chart is adapted from my book, *Media Analysis Techniques* (5th edition; 2014a), where each of the uses and gratifications is discussed in some detail. This list comes from suggested uses and gratifications made by a number of media scholars.

1. To be amused and entertained.
2. To see authority figures exalted or deflated.
3. To experience that which is beautiful.
4. To have shared experiences with others.
5. To satisfy curiosity and be informed.
6. To identify with the deity and the divine plan.
7. To find distraction and diversion.
8. To experience empathy.
9. To experience extreme emotions in a guilt-free situation.
10. To find models to identify with and to imitate.
11. To gain an identity.
12. To obtain information about the world.
13. To reinforce our belief in justice.
14. To believe in romantic love.

15. To believe in magic, the marvelous, and the miraculous.

16. To see others make mistakes.

17. To see some kind of order imposed upon the world.

18. To participate (vicariously) in history.

19. To be purged or rid of unpleasant emotions.

20. To obtain outlets for our sexual drives in a guilt-free context.

21. To explore taboo subjects with impunity.

22. To experience the ugly.

23. To affirm moral, spiritual, and cultural values.

24. To see villains in action.

Some Important Uses and Gratifications

Now I will suggest some gratifications that each genre provides, though in some cases we will see that a typical use or gratification can be supplied by a number of different genres.

Uses and Gratifications	Genres
To satisfy curiosity and be informed	Documentaries, News Shows, Talk Shows, Quiz Shows
To be amused	Situation Comedies, Comedy Shows, Musicals, Variety Shows
To identify with the deity and divine	Religious Shows, Nature Shows
To reinforce a belief in justice	Police Shows, Courtroom Dramas
To reinforce a belief in romantic love	Romance Novels, Soap Operas, Love Stories
To participate vicariously in history	Media Events, Watching Sports Like The Super Bowl, World Series

We can see that different genres provide different gratifications for people and that genres, in general, are very useful to consumers of media, who want to be able to understand what is happening in a text without having to work very hard to do so.

Uses and Gratifications and Dr. No

We can apply this list of uses and gratifications to *Dr. No*. I will offer several applications of the list to the novel and the film. When doing this kind of analysis, you must always identify something in the text that is a reflection of a particular use and gratification.

It is evident that *Dr. No* provides many gratifications for readers of the novel and for those who see the film, with its voluptuous heroine, Ursula Andress, and its famous star, Sean Connery. The book is a spy story, and its hero, James Bond, is the most popular hero in film. Even though Fleming is dead, twenty-three films have been made and others are still being made starring Fleming's hero, James Bond.

Use/Gratification	Event in *Dr. No*
To find distraction and diversion	Bond's adventures in *Dr. No*
To gain information about the world	Discussion of Jamaica's history
To reinforce a belief in justice	Dr. No is killed
To experience the ugly	Dr. No is physically repulsive
To obtain outlets for sexual drives	Bond and Honeychile make love

Psychoanalytic Criticism

Sigmund Freud

Sigmund Freud (1856–1939) is the founding father of psychoanalytic theory and one of the most influential thinkers of the twentieth century. Freud was born in Austria, was trained as a neurologist but became interested in psychological problems his patients had and developed what we know now as psychoanalytic theory. His work is controversial, and there have been many developments in psychoanalytic theory since Freud's time, but his ideas still have utility—as you shall see—when it comes to understanding works of art, the motives of characters in narrative texts, and the psyches of writers.

We have to make a distinction between psychotherapy and psychoanalytic media analysis. Psychotherapy deals with psychological problems individuals may be experiencing and uses psychoanalytic theories to help people deal with these problems. Psychoanalytic criticism involves using the psychoanalytic theories to analyze texts of all kinds. It is based, in this discussion, on Freud's pioneering work on the unconscious. As Freud explained in a book of his essays edited by Philip Rieff (1963:235–236):

> It was a triumph of the interpretative art of psychoanalysis when it succeeded in demonstrating that certain common mental acts of normal people, for which no one had hitherto attempted to put forward a psychological explanation, were to be regarded in the same light as the symptoms of neurotic: that is to say they had a *meaning*, which was unknown to the subject, but which could easily be discovered by analytic means…. A class of material was brought to light which is calculated better than any other to stimulate a belief in the existence of unconscious mental acts even in people to whom the hypothesis of something at once mental and unconscious might seem strange and even absurd. (Italics in original.)

Psychoanalytic theory is the subject of thousands of books and is a very complicated matter, but it is possible to explain some of Freud's most useful concepts for media criticism. Freud offered a general overview of the subject (Rieff 1963: 230):

> Psychoanalysis is the name (1) of a procedure for the investigation of mental processes which are almost inaccessible any other way, (2) of a method (based upon that investigation) for the treatment of neurotic disorders and (3) of a collection of psychological information obtained along those lines which is gradually being accumulated into a new scientific discipline.

For Freud, psychoanalysis is a tool that enables us to get at information buried in the unconscious that cannot be accessed in any other way. I will deal with the following topics in this discussion of psychoanalytic theory: the levels of the psyche; his structural hypothesis about the **id**, **ego**, and **superego**; the Oedipus complex; his views on symbols, and his discussion of **defense mechanisms**. As the Lesser quotation in the epigraph to this chapter points out, works of fiction often speak to our unconscious and so play a role that we frequently do not recognize.

Freud on the Unconscious

The best way to characterize Freud's views of the unconscious is to suggest our mental life can be represented by an iceberg. We know that only around 15 percent of the iceberg can be seen above the water. That represents consciousness. Just below the water line, we can see a few feet of the iceberg, and that represents our **subconscious** (or **preconscious**). But something like 80 percent of the iceberg is hidden from us, and that represents our unconscious. This drawing of an iceberg shows these relationships.

What we must recognize is that in many cases our thoughts and behaviors are shaped by material in our unconscious of which we are unaware. As Freud explained (1963:189), "What is in your mind is not identical with what you are conscious of; whether something is going on in your mind and whether you hear of it, are two different things." We are not able to control and are frequently not aware of material that is in our unconscious. Works of art, of all kinds, affect our unconscious in ways we do not understand and over which we have no control. Thus, we are not always rational in our decision making because of the hidden imperatives that come from the unconscious realms of our psyches.

As Ernest Dichter, the father of motivation research, explained in his book *The Strategy of Desire* (1960:12):

Whatever your attitude toward modern psychology or psychoanalysis, it has been proved beyond any doubt that many of our daily decisions are governed by motivations over which we have no control and of which we are often quite unaware.

We must recognize, then, that the unconscious plays an important role in our lives and much of our behavior is shaped by it. This theory of the human psyche is called the *topographic hypothesis*.

The Id, Ego, and Superego

Later in his career Freud developed another model of the human psyche, what is called his *structural hypothesis*, that involved forces he described as id, ego, and superego, which are described like this:

Id	human drives, desires, instincts: "A cauldron of seething excitement."
Ego	deals with human relations to environment, balances id and superego
Superego	human sense of guilt, conscience from parents and religion

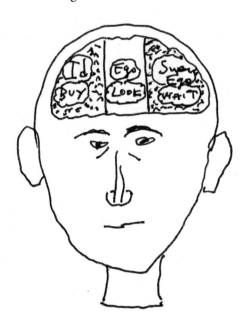

We need the id because it gives us energy and is associated with creative activities as well as desires and instincts. If we are dominated by our ids, we have a great deal of energy but lack focus and so don't accomplish very much. The ego has the task of balancing our id and superego forces. If the superego forces are dominant, we are so overwhelmed by guilt that we also don't accomplish very much. We need the superego to give us direction. It is the task of the ego to mediate between our id forces and our superego forces and find a way to ensure self-preservation by balancing them. If either id or superego becomes too dominant, we become disturbed and possibly neurotic. If we achieve a decent amount of balance between the id and superego, we are able to accomplish things of a creative or other nature. This endless conflict between id and superego elements in our psyches takes place at the unconscious level. We are generally unaware of this continuing battle.

We can use Freud's **typology** (classification system) to understand the behavior of characters in narrative texts or the nature of cities. Thus, we can suggest that gangsters and murderers in crime shows are id-dominated characters, while detectives and the police are superego figures. In *Star Trek,* Spock is an ego dominated character while Captain Kirk is a superego dominated character. The Vatican City, home of the Roman Catholic Church, is a superego city while Las Vegas is an id-dominated city. Boston and its immediate environment, with something like sixty colleges and universities, can be described as an ego city.

The Oedipus Complex and James Bond

Freud's theory about the Oedipus complex is one of his most controversial ideas. It is based upon the Greek myth of Oedipus who, not realizing what he did, killed a man (who, unknown to him was his father) and married a woman (who unknown to him was his mother). Freud's thesis was that all children go through phases in which they are strongly attached to parents of the opposite sex, and most of them move beyond it with little trouble. Those who do not master the Oedipus complex suffer from neuroses of one kind or another, because the Oedipus complex is the core of neuroses in Freudian thought. He explained his discovery of the Oedipus complex in a famous letter to his friend Wilhelm Flies on October 15, 1897:

> Being entirely honest with oneself is a good exercise. Only one idea of general value has occurred to me. I found love of the mother and jealousy of the father in my own case, too, and now believe it to be a general phenomenon of early childhood, even if it does not always occur so early as in childhood who have been made hysterics.... If that is the case, the gripping power of *Oedipus Rex,* in spite of all the rational objections to the inexorable fate that the story presupposes, becomes intelligible, and one can understand why later fate dramas were such failures. Our feelings rise against any arbitrary individual fate...but the Greek myth seizes on a compulsion which everyone recognizes because he has felt traces of it himself. Every member of the audience was once a budding Oedipus in fantasy. (quoted in Grojahn 1966:84)

Freud's argument is that audiences respond to the play *Oedipus Rex* the way they do, even if the plot is quite fantastic, because the play strikes a chord with Oedipal feelings that they have all repressed. The Oedipus complex is, Freud asserts, "general," because everyone has experienced it in childhood and then, for most people, finds a way to resolve it satisfactorily.

If the Oedipus complex is such an important factor in our psyches, it is only natural to find Oedipal themes in many texts, and some psychoanalytic media critics have found interesting examples of the Oedipus complex in films, novels, and other kinds of texts. We can return to Ian Fleming's work to find Oedipal themes in a popular text. In their book, *Bond and Beyond: the Political Career of a Popular Hero,* Tony Bennett and Janet Woollacott discuss Bond's Oedipal problems. They write (1987:125–126):

> In *You Only Live Twice,* Bond is going through a peculiarly acute phase in his ever-ongoing, never-to-be-resolved Oedipal crisis. Indeed, between them, *You Only Live Twice* and its sequel *The Man with the Golden Gun* offer a fairly explicit rehearsal of the Oedipus myth. Bond is sent away to a foreign land, is given another name, loses his memory so that like Oedipus, he lacks a knowledge of his true identity and parentage, eventually leaves those who have adopted him (Kissy) and journeys back to his homeland where (having been captured and brainwashed by the KGB *en route*) he attempts, in the opening pages of *The Man with the Golden Gun,* to kill M.

Bond, as the authors point out, is continually threatened with symbolic castration by the powerful figures that capture him in various adventures. In *Dr. No,* we find that No hated his father, suggesting that he, too, had Oedipal problems.

Bennett and Woollacott suggest that we find these Oedipal themes in the Bond adventures because, it can be suggested, Fleming had not resolved his own Oedipal problems; he was excessively fond of his mother and didn't like his father. In Bond's novel and films, he inevitably meets and is attracted to a beautiful woman, whom we may see as being an idealized version of his mother. Later, a powerful and older male figure, a symbolic father, captures Bond and plans to castrate him and then kill him. Bond always finds a way to escape and kill the villain and then is able to have a sexual relationship with the woman.

We can find the Oedipus complex or Oedipal themes in many texts. This can be explained relatively easily. If Freud is correct about the Oedipus complex, everyone experiences it, and residues of this experience then still exist in the unconscious of the writers of the Bond film scripts, the film makers of the Bond stories, and all the people who read the Bond novels and see the Bond films. From a psychoanalytic perspective, we can say that one reason we are drawn to stories of all kinds in all media is that, although we don't recognize what is happening, these stories either help us resolve our Oedipal problems or confirm that we have resolved them.

One reason James Bond may be popular, I would suggest, is because his Oedipal problems somehow speak to and resonate, at the unconscious level, with those of his fans, some of whom have not completely resolved their Oedipal problems for one reason or another. Bennett and Woollacott explain the Oedipal themes in the Bond stories—symbolic castration when M takes Bond's gun away from him in *Dr. No* and in other films, Bond's being captured by powerful, older men who threaten real castration and death, and so on—by discussing Fleming's psyche. They write (1987:128):

> The novels have been regarded as an expression of Fleming's own unresolved infantile psycho-drama—his excessive fondness for his mother, his hostility towards his father, his generally contemptuous attitudes towards women and his preference for male companions being interpreted as a sign of his failure to pass through the castration anxiety of the Oedipal phase to assume a position of genitally-centered, female-directed sexuality.

What we find in the Bond stories, then, is an endlessly varied reflection of Fleming's psychological problems. It is reasonable to assume that the Bond stories appeal, in unconscious ways, to people who may have similar problems—though perhaps not to the same degree that is found in Fleming's life. He seems to have overcompensated for his Oedipal problems by having numerous affairs with women, even though he was married.

Woshington Monument

An American
phallic symbol.

Symbols in Psychoanalytic Theory

Symbols are kinds of signs in that they stand for other things and their meaning always has to be learned. They can stand for any number of things—ideas, institutions, body parts, and so on. They play a role in our psyches because they are often used to mask ideas, thoughts, and actions that we want to keep hidden. They play a particularly important role in our dreams, where they disguise certain aggressive impulses and sexual desires that would disturb our dream censors and wake us.

Freud's theories about symbols focus on their sexual nature. In essence, we disguise sexual desires in our dreams by using symbols that trick our dream censors, which allows us to continue dreaming. Here is what Freud had to say about the sexual identity of symbols. He writes (1953:161–162):

> The male genital organ is symbolically represented in dreams in many different ways.... Its more conspicuous and, to both sexes, more interesting part, the penis, is symbolized primarily by objects which resemble it in form, being long and upstanding, such as *sticks, umbrellas, poles, trees,* and the like; also by objects which, like the thing symbolized, have the property of penetration, and consequently of injuring the body—that is to say pointed weapons of all sorts: *knives, daggers, lances, sabres;* firearms are similarly used: *guns, pistols, and revolvers.*

There are other items, Freud adds, that function as **phallic symbols**, such as objects from which water flows and objects that can raise themselves up, mirroring erections in males. These symbols all are tied to what he calls wish fulfillment and the desire of men to be with women.

Unlike men, whose sexual organs are symbolized by penetrating objects, women are represented by incorporative objects. Freud explains (1953:163–164):

The female genitals are symbolically represented by all such objects as share with them the property of enclosing a space or are capable of acting as receptacles: such as *pits, hollows, and caves,* and also *jars and bottles,* and *boxes* of all sorts and sizes, *chests, coffers, pockets,* and so forth. *Ships,* too, come into this category. Many symbols refer rather to the uterus than to the other genital organs: thus *cupboards, stoves,* and above all, *rooms.* Room symbolism here links up with that of houses, whilst *doors and gates* represent the genital opening.

There are other phenomena, such as woods and thickets (symbols of pubic hair) and jewel cases, that also are feminine symbols.

Freud cautioned that you can't assume every object that is long and thin and penetrating is a phallic symbol when he is reported to have said, "Sometimes a cigar is just a cigar." This means that Freud recognized that a cigar is not always a phallic symbol. But we must recall that if "sometimes a cigar is just a cigar," sometimes a cigar is *not* just a cigar. Freudian psychoanalytic theory suggests that in our dreams we camouflage our id-based sexual desires by using symbols. This prevents the superego elements in our psyches, what we can call the "dream censor," from recognizing the sexual nature of our dreams and waking us up. In narrative texts, we can find actual symbolic objects, symbolic words, symbolic names of characters, symbolic actions, symbolic buildings and spaces all mixed together, and it is the task of the readers of literary texts or viewers of films and videos to recognize the symbols and interpret their significance.

The Defense Mechanisms

The ego makes use of various defense mechanisms to deal with id-based instincts and control super-ego based anxieties and guilt feelings. This occurs mostly at the unconscious level and involves actions that control both id and superego elements of our psyches. Below I list and briefly describe some of the more common defense mechanisms. This list is useful in that it helps us understand the motivations of characters in texts. These defense mechanisms, such as **rationalization**, are found in the unconscious of the writers of texts and communicate directly with the unconscious of the readers or viewers of texts.

Ambivalence	Feelings of love and hate or other oppositional attitudes towards a person or object.
Avoidance	Refusing to admit to consciousness certain disturbing feelings or beliefs.
Denial	Blocking from consciousness something that is disturbing.
Fixation	Obsessive attachment to something, generally caused by traumatic experience.
Identification	Desire to be like someone in some way.
Projection	Projecting negative feelings we have about ourselves onto someone else.
Rationalization	Offering a justification generated by unconscious forces for things we do.
Reaction Formation	Dealing with opposing attitudes by suppressing one.
Regression	Returning to an earlier stage in our development to deal with anxiety and stress.
Repression	Barring unconscious instincts and desires from our consciousness. (Basic defense mechanism.)
Suppression	Putting painful thoughts out of mind.

Having dealt with Freud's theories about the psyche and the unconscious, let me move on to another important thinker whose ideas have had an enormous historical impact—Karl Marx.

Marxist Ideological Analysis

Karl Marx

Karl Marx was born in Trier, Germany, in 1818 and died in London in 1883. He is buried in Highgate Cemetery. Marx's ideas are behind the development of communism, which is now generally discredited, but his ideas are also useful for media scholars since his writings can be applied to understanding the role of media in society. Marxist theory, like semiotic theory, psychoanalytic theory, and sociological theory, is a very complex matter about which thousands of books and articles have been written. There are 2,520,000 sites that come up when you type Marxism on Google (as of August 13, 2014), so obviously Marxism is a subject of widespread interest. Although Marxism as an economic doctrine has been repudiated, **Marxism** is very useful as a method for analyzing **cultures**, societies, and communications of all kinds. In this discussion of Marxist analysis, I will deal with four of the more important elements of the theory: alienation, **dialectical materialism**, **class conflict**, and **false consciousness**. There are approximately 11,000 books on various aspects of Marxism sold at Amazon.com books, so it is a subject of considerable popularity.

Let me begin by offering an overview of Marxist theory and its relation to media, popular culture, and related concerns. In his article, "Mass Culture, Political Consciousness, and English Studies," Donald Lazere offers us an excellent introduction to the way Marxists deal with cultural phenomena (1977: 755–756):

> Applied to any aspect of culture, Marxist method seeks to explicate the manifest and latent or coded reflections of modes of material production, ideological values, class relations and structures of social power—racial or sexual as well as politico-economic—or the state of consciousness of people in a precise historical or socio-economic situation. The Marxist method, recently in varying degrees of combination with structuralism and semiology, has provided an incisive analytic tool for studying the political signification in every

facet of contemporary culture, including popular entertainment in TV and films, music, mass circulation books, newspaper and magazine features, comics, fashion, tourism, sports and games, as well as such acculturating institutions as education, religion, the family and child-rearing, social and sexual relations between men and women—all the patterns of work, play, and other customs of everyday life. The most frequent theme in Marxist cultural criticism is the way the prevalent mode of production and the **ideology** of the ruling class in any society dominate every phase of culture, and at present, the way capitalist production and ideology dominate American culture, along with that of the rest of the world that American business and culture have colonized. This domination is perpetuated both through overt propaganda in political rhetoric, news reporting, advertising and public relations, and through the often unconscious absorption of capitalistic values by creators and consumers in all the above aspects of the culture of everyday life.

We can see, then, that Marxist criticism covers many different aspects or "facets" of any society or culture. What we find when we adopt a Marxist perspective is that there is a political dimension to all kinds of things that we never thought of as political.

Alienation

Alienation, which literally means "no ties" or "no connections," is perhaps the core concept of the Marxist analysis of capitalist or bourgeois societies. We also find the term "alien" as part of alienation. Aliens are strangers in any society. We see examples of alienation in many television programs and films, in which characters somehow do not "fit in." Dr. No is an excellent example of an alienated person. His very name suggests negativity. Marx argues that although capitalist economies can produce great number of goods, people in these societies feel separated from others and alienated from themselves, as well. In bourgeois societies, workers are estranged and separated from their true interests and work only to earn money, which will then enable them to participate in consumption. As Marx explains (1964:169–170):

The worker...feels himself at home only during his leisure, whereas at work he feels homeless. His work is not voluntary but imposed, *forced labour*. It is not the satisfaction of a need, but only a *means* for satisfying other needs. Its alien character is clearly shown by the fact that as soon as there is no physical or other compulsion it is avoided like the plague.... The *alienation* of the worker in his product means not only that his labour becomes an object, takes on its own existence, but that it exists outside him, independently, and alien to him, and that it stands opposed to him as an autonomous power. The life which he has given to the objects sets itself against him as an alien and hostile force.

What happens, then, is that workers become estranged, not only from their work, but from their friends, from themselves, and from their communities. They become, finally, prisoners of their alienated needs and end up, Marx writes, as "*self-conscious* and *self-acting* commodities." But it isn't only the workers who are alienated in capitalist societies. For Marx, everyone in capitalist societies is alienated, for those who are members of the ruling classes are alienated from themselves and from the working classes, whom they exploit.

For Marxists, it is alienation that generates consumer cultures, for it is only when people purchase things that they find momentary gratifications and escape from the alienation that plagues them. There is a vicious cycle at work here. Workers in capitalist countries are exploited and feel alienated, and the more they work the more alienated they feel. They escape from this feeling of alienation by buying things and participating in consumer culture, but this costs money, so ironically, they are forced to work harder and harder to escape to be able to keep on purchasing things to escape from the effects of their work.

Dialectical Materialism

The materialism that Marx talked about was not a psychological feeling, tied to greed, that people have that they want to have as many of the "good" things in life as they can, which places them as members of consumer cultures. Marx wrote about *dialectical* materialism, a philosophical position, which involves the way a society organizes itself. He wrote about this topic in his "Preface to a Contribution to the Critique of Political Economy." He begins by discussing the relationship that exists between society and consciousness (Bottomore 1964:51):

> In the social production which men carry on they enter into definite relations that are indispensable and independent of their will; these relations of production correspond to a definite state of development of their material powers of production. The totality of these relations of production constitutes the economic structure of society—the real foundation, on which legal and political superstructures arise and to which definite forms of social consciousness correspond. The mode of production of material life determines the general character of the social, political and spiritual processes of life. It is not the consciousness of men that determines their being, but, on the contrary, their social being determines their consciousness.

The economic system, the base, shapes what he called the superstructure, which is made up of the basic institutions of society: our legal system, our educational system, our family system, and all the other systems found in a given society. Our "social being," he concludes, shapes our "consciousness." The economic system of a society affects the ideas that individuals have, and these ideas play an important role in determining the kinds of institutions they will establish.

Marxists argue that the ruling classes, which control our media, have the ability to shape our consciousness. Marxists, and others, point out that the continual consolidation of the media leads to situations in which a small number of people, who own the media, can shape our consciousness.

Marx also wrote about the roles individuals play in this process. As he explains in "The German Ideology" (Bottomore 1964:74–75):

> The production of ideas, of conceptions, of consciousness, is at first directly interwoven with the material activity and the material intercourse of men, the language of real life. Conceiving, thinking, the mental intercourse of men, appear at this stage as the direct efflux from their

material behavior. The same applies to mental production as expressed in the language of politics, laws, morality, religion, and metaphysics of a people. Men are the producers of their conceptions, ideas, etc.—real, active men, as they are conditioned by the definite development of their productive forces and of the intercourse corresponding to these, up to its furthest forms. Consciousness can never be anything else than conscious existence.

This passage brings people into the picture and suggests that although consciousness is socially produced, one of the basic concepts of materialism, it is always filtered through the minds of individuals and is not something that works automatically. This means that individuals can, in some cases, gain an understanding of their situation (and for Marx this would be a recognition of the proletariat's exploitation by the ruling classes) and, by organizing, make changes for the better.

The Ruling Class

Class Conflict

Marx argued that all Capitalist societies are based upon class conflict, between the working classes, or proletariat, and the ruling classes, who own the means of production. History, for Marx, is the record of endless class conflict—until, that is, the establishment of a communist society, in which classes disappear and, with them, conflict. Let me quote from T. B. Bottomore's collection of Marx's writings, *Selected Writings in Sociology and Social Philosophy* (1964:200):

> The history of all hitherto existing society is the history of class struggles. Freeman and slave, patrician and plebeian, lord and serf, guild-master and journeyman, in a word oppressor and oppressed, stood in constant opposition to one another, carried on an uninterrupted, now hidden, now open fight, a fight that each time ended either in a revolutionary reconstitution of society at large, or in the common ruin of the contending classes.

The ruling classes try to avert class conflict by indoctrinating the masses of workers with "ruling class ideas," such as the notion that the differences in classes found in capitalist societies are natural and not historical. If they are natural, nothing can be done to change them. Marxists argue that the economic arrangements found in bourgeois societies, in which a small number of people are very wealthy and large numbers of people are increasingly poor, is a historical matter and thus can be changed—by adopting communism and getting rid of classes. Most Marxist scholars, I should point out, do not believe in the need for revolution but use his ideas to critique capitalist or "bourgeois" societies.

False Consciousness

It is important for the ruling class to affect people's consciousness by giving them certain ideas; in this way the wealthy, who benefit most from the social arrangements in a capitalist country, maintain the status quo. Marx describes how the ruling class operates (Bottomore 1964:78):

> The ideas of the ruling class are, in every age, the ruling ideas: i. e., the class which is the dominant *material* force in society is at the same time its dominant *intellectual* force. The class which has the means of material production at its disposal, has control at the same time over the means of mental production, so that in consequence the ideas of those who lack the means of mental production are, in general, subject to it. The dominant ideas are nothing more than the ideal expression of the dominant material relationships, the dominant material relationships grasped as ideas, and thus of the relationships which make one class the ruling one; they are consequently the ideas of its dominance. The individuals composing the ruling class possess among other things consciousness, and therefore think. Insofar, therefore, as they rule as a class and determine the whole extent of an epoch, it is self-evident that they do this in their whole range and thus, among other things, rule also as thinkers, as producers of ideas, and regulate the production and distribution of the ideas of their age. Consequently their ideas are the ruling ideas of their age.

Thus, for Marx, the dominant ideas in a society are those popularized by the ruling class in its own interest. Generally speaking, the ruling classes believe their own messages, because these classes have the services of a group of conceptualizing ideologists (writers, journalists, etc.) who, as Marx puts it, "make it their chief source of livelihood to develop and perfect the illusions of the class about itself" (Bottomore 1964:79). Marxists argue that the American dream, which shapes the thinking of many Americans (or used to before we became aware of the amount of inequality here), is part of our consciousness because it is found as a subtext in many of our entertainments.

We can see this in this analysis of *Dr. No* that follows.

Applying Marxist Theory to *Dr. No*

Like the other methodologies discussed above, Marxism can be applied to many aspects of American (or any other) society, and many literary critics, social scientists and other kinds of scholars, use Marxism, often in combination with semiotics and psychoanalytic theory, in analyzing texts, social behavior, and other cultural phenomena. We can apply Marxist theories to *Dr. No* and the James Bond character.

In Tony Bennett and Janet Woollacott's *Bond and Beyond: The Political Career of a Popular Hero,* we read that Fleming has used Bond to place England in the "center" of the world stage, and his exploits help it maintain that position. Thus, England, a first world country, becomes the dominant focus of our attention, and third world countries, as represented by places like Jamaica, are of marginal interest. Bond, the hero of "imperialist spy-thrillers," the authors explain (1987:99), "can be read as a hero of the NATO alliance."

Part of Bond's appeal is based on his elite socio-economic class and the way he affirms the value of English public schools—that is, very expensive schools for elite elements of English society. He is not upper-class like many of the other heroes of British spy fiction, but he is well off. Bennett and Woollacott describe Bond as a member of the international "new elite" (1987:112):

> His social views are, of course, anything but egalitarian. His attitudes toward trade unions are (or should be) unprintable and when, on one occasion, he encounters a member of the British working class who does not conform to the model of a faithful old retainer—a fly young taxi-driver—he regards his teddy-boy appearance as "typical of the cheap self-assertiveness of young labour since the war (*Thunderball,* p. 16). Unequivocally committed to elite values, Bond seeks to distinguish himself from the common mass—by the Bentley

convertible he drives, his special cigarettes and hand tailored suits. But his elitism lacks the usual class articulation of the hero of the earlier imperialist spy thriller. His attitudes toward sex, gambling and pleasure are distinctly liberal and his tastes and lifestyle have a decidedly international and cosmopolitan flavor.

The fact that Bond is, in terms of the number of films made, the most popular hero in films offers us a good example of how bourgeois ideas can fascinate—and Marxists would say deceive and indoctrinate—the masses. Let me suggest that Bond's image has changed in recent films. For example, in *Skyfall*, the twenty-third Bond film, he is played by Daniel Craig, who has a middle class persona and is not upper class and aristocratic like earlier Bonds.

In the early Bond films, he is portrayed as a "connoisseur" whose fastidiousness and curious tics—martinis shaken and not stirred—distracts us from the fact that he is a consumer extraordinaire, who has expensive clothes, drives an expensive car, visits the most expensive and desirable tourist sites, and "consumes" beautiful and exotic women in the course of his adventures. Some writers have suggested that his taste is not really refined and that what he presents to readers of Bond novels and viewers of Bond films is the illusion of good taste, not good taste itself. For Marxists, it is his function as a role model for many men that is so disturbing.

Applied Analysis: Interpreting a Text

I use the term analysis rather than criticism most of the time because the term "criticism" has negative connotations. In addition, the analysis we make is not of media per se, which is what we find in Marshall McLuhan's book, *Understanding Media,* but of a mass-mediated text of some kind. When people say they are going to watch television, they mean they are going to watch certain programs on television, and these programs are generally ones that can be classified as coming under certain genres: sports contests, talent shows, reality shows, crime shows, and so on, as I explained earlier.

The best way to visualize what textual analysis involves is to imagine four professors sitting around a very large round table. Each professor represents a different perspective on studying mass mediated texts. We find a semiotician, a sociologist, a psychoanalyst, and a Marxist. In the middle of the table is a text: an advertisement, a film, a novel, a televised basketball game, or a joke. We have only covered four of these theoretical models in this chapter, but there are others.

In recent years, we have come to recognize that all disciplines have limitations; that explains why there is so much interest, now, in multi-disciplinary, trans-disciplinary, or interdisciplinary approaches to topics of interest to scholars. When we come to the arts and to the mysteries of creativity, the limitations of single disciplinary approaches become quite apparent. Is it their psyches/personalities or the social milieus in which the artists live or their family backgrounds or events of great importance that explain their creative work?

Applications

1. How and why do people "lie" with signs? Include in your discussion impostors and cross-dressers.

2. Make a list of the uses and gratifications people obtain from a television series. Are there other uses and gratifications you can think of that explain why people are attracted to certain texts?

3. Use Freudian theory to analyze a text, chosen by you or assigned by your professor. What insights does Freudian theory supply that other methods of textual analysis ignore?

4. Find some examples of false consciousness within American culture. How is it that Americans don't see them?

Chapter 4

Communication, Identity, and Culture

Messages: An Introduction to Communication by Arthur Asa Berger, 88–99.

"Yes, impostors! That's the word. My theories really bother my colleagues because they tend to look at human beings in aggregates, as members of society or some class or culture or sub-culture. So they can talk about things like behavior in crowds or American identity—whatever that might be—or various ideological positions, that still deal with large groups of people—women, gays, people of color, the proletariat. You name it. My focus, since I have a psychoanalytic approach to things, deals with individuals and how they achieve their identities. Or don't achieve them, since many people, as my theory suggests, are pretenders to an identity."

"I don't understand how that can happen?" said Hunter. "Jean-Marie said that in postmodern societies people often change their identities to suit their whims, but that doesn't seem to me to be the same thing as pretending to have an identity or being an impostor."

Duerfklein smiled, knowingly.

"You must remember that the term 'personality' is based on the Latin root 'persona' which means mask. So our personalities are, it can be said, masks that we create to deal with others in social situations. You might contrast one's personality with what might be called one's character or 'self,' one's true being. What I argue, based on my work with numerous patients, is that many people never grow up, never cast off immature notions and fantasies of what it means to be an adult, never achieve coherence and continuity in their sense of themselves, so what you get, ultimately, is a fake person, a simulation, a fraud. And these people can't help themselves because they don't even recognize that they are impostors. They've devoted all their energy to fooling others and they end up also fooling themselves."

"What did Socrates tell people to do? 'Know thyself,' he said. It isn't easy to do. Also, these impostors suffer from a kind of amnesia, especially about their childhoods, when many of the foundations for their identities were established, and their adolescent periods, when they were searching desperately for acceptable identities. They forget who they were, so they are condemned to continually creating new characters for themselves. It's rather sad."

In this chapter I argue that what we describe as culture can be thought of a collection of codes particular to where we were brought up and where we live. That helps explain why the French way of life is so different from the American way of life and why both are so different from the Japanese way of life. If you see a charming film like *Amelie,* which is steeped in French culture, you can see how different life in France is from life in the United States.

I deal in this chapter with the work of Clotaire Rapaille on national codes, my theories about **culture codes**, a discussion of how cultural codes shape conversation, and work by sociologist Orrin Klapp on codes and identity. The quotation in the epigraph comes from an academic mystery I wrote, *Mistake in Identity,* which deals with different perspectives on identity. A psychoanalyst, Sigfried Duerfklein, has a theory that we are all impostors and don't really know who we are.

When we travel and are exposed to different ways of life, we experience what is called "culture shock." We become somewhat disoriented because people in foreign countries do things differently from the way we do them: they eat at different times, they eat different foods, they work different hours, and so on. One of the terms scholars use to describe structured behavior in any culture is "code," which stands for rules we obey. I introduced this topic in a number of chapters in this book. For example, I deal with Umberto Eco's ideas about aberrant decoding and Bernstein's work on different language codes. The way we understand these codes is tied to our socioeconomic classes, and they help shape our identities and sense of possibility. The important thing to remember is that we have to learn these codes—we are not born with them. We learn some of them from the way our parents and others speak to us and some of them by observing how people behave. Codes, we find, are intimately connected to the communication process. You aren't born knowing codes—you have to learn them. Someone teaches you them or you observe things and figure out the codes for yourself. We must also remember that we are unaware of many of these codes; they are in our unconscious or are seen as something natural or that "goes without saying."

Clotaire Rapaille on the Culture Code

Clotaire Rapaille is a French psychoanalyst and marketing consultant whose book, *The Culture Code: An Ingenious Way to Understand Why People Around the World Live and Buy as They Do*, explores the different codes of behavior and taste that countries such as Japan, France, Britain, and the United States imprint on children. As he writes (2006:21), "Most of us imprint the meanings of the things most central to our lives by the age of seven. This is because emotion is the central force for children under the age of seven." He

Clotaire Rapaille

explains (2006:6), "Once an imprint occurs, it strongly conditions our thought processes and shapes our future action. Each imprint helps make us more of who we are. The combination of imprints defines us."

Rapaille argues that our behavior is shaped by three kinds of unconscious: a Freudian *individual* unconscious, a Jungian *collective* unconscious (Swiss psychiatrist Carl Jung's theories deal with archetypes which, he claims, are universal themes found in myths, religions, and works of art), and Rapaille's own *cultural* unconscious, which represents the national codes imprinted on us that shape our behavior. He explains the relationship that exists between codes and imprints (2006:11):

Carl Jung

> An imprint and its Code are like a lock and its combination. If you have all the right numbers in the right sequence, you can open the lock. Doing so over a vast array of imprints has profound implications. It brings to us the answer to one of our most fundamental questions: why do we act the way we do? Understanding the Culture Code provides us with a remarkable new tool—a new set of glasses, if you will, with which to view ourselves and our behaviors. It changes the way we see everything

around us. What's more, it confirms what we have always suspected is true—that, despite our common humanity, people around the world really are different. The Culture Code offers a way to understand how.

So, by the age of seven children in different cultures have different notions of what is a good meal, how one relates to certain foods, and a number of other things that are specific to certain countries. One fascinating discussion in his book involves the way American and French people relate to cheese.

C H E E S E

According to Rapaille, cheese is "dead" in the American code, and so Americans wrap cheese in plastic and store it in "morgues" known as refrigerators. But cheese is "alive" for the French, and so they store their cheese in containers (cloches) that are not refrigerated. For Rapaille, every country has its codes, and finding the codes that inform each country helps us understand why people buy what they buy and live as they do. The matter of codes as a means of understanding behavior is, it turns out, something I have been interested in for many years.

We must recognize that codes are culturally acquired, which means that they are communicated to us by others— parents, priests, peers, and pop culture. These codes vary not only nationally but regionally and locally. They are shaped by matters such as our gender, race, religion, ethnicity, and socio-economic class. This means that though Americans share many national codes, they also have different subcodes. We have many different accents in America, from the Bostonian accent (I'm a Bostonian and people can tell I'm from Boston even though I've been away from Boston for more than sixty years) to the Southerner's "y'all."

Arthur Asa Berger on Culture Codes

My own book, *Culture Codes*, deals with the way that codes inform many different aspects of daily life. I wrote the book many years ago but only published it in 2012. As I explained in the book (2012: 7):

> In this book I suggest that cultures can be thought of as collections of codes that shape our behavior. Codes that we are aware of we call "mores" or "rules" or "laws," but codes that we do not recognize, but which shape our thinking and behavior in many areas, I call *culture codes*. I explain the various characteristics of these codes below. We know that genetic codes play a major role in shaping our physical bodies and in many illnesses we are plagued with. In the same light, *culture codes* play a major role in our thoughts and behavior, even though we generally are not aware of the existence of these codes.

I can offer an example of the way culture codes by talking about steak. In American culture, we believe there are only two basic ways to properly cook steak: we grill steaks over charcoal or we broil them. Nobody in the United States, or anywhere in the world, boils steak—as far as I know.

People lower down the socio-economic ladder usually like their steaks well done (a restaurateur told me this), and people high up on the social ladder tend to like them rare. In the course of wandering around the world and visiting fifty countries in the last sixty years, I've never been at a restaurant where boiled steak was served. Also, I've never seen boiled steak in a cookbook. As we grow up in America and watch the way our parents cook and eat steaks and the way steaks are served in restaurants, we learn how to think about steak—how to cook it and how to eat it. Traditionally, we serve salads with steak dinners. In the United States, salad is served before the main course; in France, it is generally served after the main course.

We internalize the rules we learn as we grow up and they tend to guide us for the rest of our lives, though there are times when people rebel against their culture codes and switch to a different set of culture codes. These culture codes shape our attitudes towards romantic love, beauty, work, notions about the good life, and many other things. It is when we travel and are exposed to culture codes in other countries that we begin to recognize and then, perhaps, question our national and regional culture codes and consider adopting certain codes from other cultures.

One Hundred Percent American

I should point out that we have already adopted many things from other countries. In a famous article, "100 Percent American," by Ralph Linton, we read:

> There can be no question about the average American's Americanism or his desire to preserve this precious heritage at all costs. Nevertheless, some insidious foreign ideas have already wormed their way into his civilization without his realizing what was going on. Thus dawn finds the unsuspecting patriot garbed in pajamas, a garment of East Indian

origin; and lying in a bed built on a pattern which originated in either Persia or Asia Minor. He is muffled to the ears in un-American materials: cotton, first domesticated in India; linen, domesticated in the Near East; wool from an animal native to Asia Minor; or silk whose uses were first discovered by the Chinese. All these substances have been transformed into cloth by methods invented in Southwestern Asia. If the weather is cold enough he may even be sleeping under an eiderdown quilt invented in Scandinavia. (1937:427)

Linton's article goes on to deal with many other supposedly "100 percent American" objects that originated in foreign lands. All cultures borrow from one another, as any American who finds McDonald's hamburger restaurants in many foreign countries and drinks Italian Espresso coffees at Starbucks knows.

We see, then, that what we describe as culture can be seen as a collection of codes that we learn (or, in Rapaille's term, are "imprinted" on us) as we grow up in a culture or subculture that shapes our thinking and behavior. One thing that social scientists do is search for the codes of which people are unaware but which play an important role in their lives.

Given the fact that cultures are so different, it is reasonable to assume that countries differ in the rules for conversing and other aspects of the communication process. Implicit in my discussion of Rapaille's book and my book is the notion that much of our identity is shaped by our nationalities. Rapaille offers a fascinating description of dinners in Japan, China, and England. Japanese families, he explains, don't eat dinner together. Japanese men work all day and then go out to drink and eat with their friends. Japanese children are served well before their fathers come home, and when Japanese couples go out to eat, the men and women eat separately. In China, food is cooked in various places in a home. When the food is served, Chinese people focus on eating and don't talk to one another very much. Even at business dinners, there may be a spirited conversation about something, but when the food is served, conversation stops and everyone feasts. In England, dinners are very formal and there are rules of behavior involving such things as how one sits, how cutlery is to be used, and how one chews. The English do not offer a taste of food on their plates to others (which is common in America) since they regard this as vulgar and unsanitary.

All of these behavior codes are learned. They are imprinted on young children by their parents, who teach them certain codes, and this behavior is reinforced by the various communications to which children are exposed—from their parents and from the culture and popular culture in which they grow up.

What Do You Do for a Living?

Knowing the codes by which people eat and the other codes that shape their thinking and behavior is important if you are marketing (which we will understand to mean various forms of persuasive communication) products to them; different countries require different approaches. Rapaille is a marketer, and knowing Japanese codes was crucial to him if he was to be able to convince the Japanese to drink coffee—they didn't before he taught Nestlé's how to develop an interest in coffee in Japan. If you're dealing with Americans whose code, Rapaille explains, is "work is who you are," you have to send them messages in advertising that are congruent with this notion, while for the French, who value pleasure more than work, you have to deal with that aspect of the French national character in advertising.

Isn't it interesting that in America, when we meet people for the first time, it doesn't take them very long to ask, "What do you do?" In America, if Rapaille is correct, that question is pivotal, since we believe that "work is who you are." In France, that question might not be asked so quickly (or at all), because the French don't believe work is who they are—that one's work defines one's identity.

Then there are regional considerations that help shape our identities. Growing up in Boston is different from growing up in Dallas; that is, regions of a country have their particular codes which play a role in the way we form our identities. The food people eat in the South is different, in various ways, from food people eat on the West Coast. And people's accents, along with many other things, are different in different regions. Thus, in the United States, Northerners generally speak more quickly than Southerners, and people from different ethnic groups vary in terms of what they feel is the proper distance between speakers and the number and kind of gestures they make when speaking.

We now recognize that America has become a multi-ethnic, multi-racial country with large numbers of people from other countries living here, and with many different races, native languages, and food preferences. There are also significant class differences found in America, with a relatively small number of people at the top of the income totem-pole and large numbers of people at the bottom. All of these differences are manifested in the way people speak, the languages they speak at home, in the language codes they use, and in the many codes that shape their identities. If I were to use a metaphor to describe America now, I would say we are like a beef stew—with different ingredients (groups of one kind or another) in the pot maintaining their identities and not blending into some kind of an all-mixed together "melting pot" soup.

The Collective Search for Identity

In addition to nationalities and regions, there are many other factors involved in shaping our identities, like the groups to which we belong: do we belong to an orchestra that plays classical music or a band of hip hop or jazz musicians? And, of course, there are physical matters, like our race, body type, hair color, height, and there are cultural, demographic, and psychographic factors, such as our religion, education, socio-economic class (which affects our  "life chances"), occupation, place of residence (and how often our parents have moved), where we live, personality, and the sub-cultures to which we are exposed and become part of.

Orrin Klapp, a sociologist, wrote a fascinating book called *The Collective Search for Identity,* which focused on the many ways in which people use groups of one kind or another to help find a suitable identity. He describes the book in his Preface (1969:vii):

This book is about identity-seeking movements of modern society. It deals with such things as fashions, fads, poses, ritual, cultic movements, recreation, heroes and celebrities, and crusades from the point of view of what they tell about the identity search of a mass society. My view, briefly, is that a collective identity search is symptomatic of the fact that some modern social systems deprive people of psychological "payoffs," the lack of which, expressed by terms such as alienation, meaninglessness, identity problem, motivates a mass groping for activities and symbols with which to restore or find a new identity. People grope because they do not really know what is wrong, especially when there is physical prosperity *yet* a sense of being cheated. When mass movements become concerned with identity, they develop certain characteristics such as "ego-screaming," concern with costume and self-ornamentation, style rebellion, concern with emotional gestures rather than practical effects, adulation of heroes, cultism, and the like.... Young people may view the opportunities and careers laid out for them by parents and say, "Not for me." I have chosen to examine in this book then, certain activities which plainly show a turning away from "sensible" economic and political measures toward a search for meaning to oneself, for oneself, in oneself.

Though this book was written many years ago, Klapp's discussion of the problems people having in achieving a satisfying identity seems very contemporary. Our search for identity is something personal, but when you multiply all the people engaged in that search, it becomes a social phenomenon of considerable importance. Klapp wrote another book, *Heroes, Victims and Fools*, in which he argues that Americans obtain their personal identities by identifying with one of a large number of variations on the three basic personality types in his title. Many of the heroes, victims and fools he discussed were tied to celebrities and famous actors and actresses, who functioned, we may say, as role models.

This analysis of culture and communication and the codes that shape our behavior sets the stage for our next chapter, which deals with interpersonal communication, the way people converse with one another. Where people are raised and the imprints that have shaped their personalities play an important role in the way they communicate with others.

Applications

1. You've learned from Rapaille how American culture shapes the way we relate to cheese. Pick another type of food to which American cultural codes apply. Explain why.

2. Describe some cultural codes that American children learn during their first seven years.

3. What is the relationship between socio-economic class and codes? Consider factors such as gender and race in answering this question.

4. We've discussed the significance of asking people, "What do you do for a living?" Make a list of some of the other questions people typically ask one another in conversations and analyze their significance and meaning.

5. What do you make of Sigfried Duerfklein's theory that we are all impostors? Apply it to yourself and some people you know. Do impostors always know they are impostors? Explain your answers.

Interpersonal Communication

When persons engage in regulated dealings with each other, they come to employ social routines or practices, namely, patterned adaptations to the rules—including conformances, by-passings, secret deviations, excusable infractions, flagrant violations, and the like. These variously motivated and variously functioning patterns of actual behavior, these routines associated with ground rules, together constitute what might be called a "social order."

Erving Goffman, *Relations in Public*

Prisoner: Where am I?

Number Two: In The Village.

Prisoner: What do you want?

Number Two: Information.

Prisoner: Which side are you on?

Number Two: That would be telling. We want information, information, information....

Prisoner: You won't get it.

Number Two: By hook or by crook we will.

Prisoner: Who are you?

Number Two: The new Number Two.

Prisoner: Who is Number One?

Number Two: You are Number Six.

Prisoner: I am not a number! I am a free man.

Number Two: (Laughing hysterically) Ha, ha, ha, ha....

Beginnings of episodes of *The Prisoner*

What people say to one another when they meet—the words they use and the expressiveness of their language—is only the tip of the iceberg. There are a large number of things, hidden away and in our unconscious, that help us understand why people say what they say to one another. I will deal with some of the complexities involved in interpersonal communication, which I will divide into two areas: verbal communication and **nonverbal communication**, both of which play a role in interpersonal communication. I deal with nonverbal communication is greater detail in Chapter 9. I also discuss the structure of conversations, as explained by Johnson and Lakoff in their book, *Metaphors We Live By*. Then I discuss typical topics of conversation and matters, such as voice quality, posture, and eye contact, that affect conversations. I conclude with a number of factors, such as **demographics**, context, and social roles, that play an important role in interpersonal conversation.

In the epigraph I quoted Erving Goffman, one of the most remarkable sociologists of recent years, who explains that there are certain rules that govern our behavior when we communicate with one another—social routines and rules that we often violate one way or another. Language use is, after all, based on certain rules of grammar, and there are also rules and conventions that we are expected to obey, just as we are expected to obey the rules of the road when we drive.

The dialogue from "The Prisoner," a sci-fi spy television series of the late sixties that had a cult following, took place at the beginning of each episode. It always involved Patrick McGoohan, the actor who played Number Six, and the person in charge of the island where he had been brought (after being gassed in the first episode, when he resigned from the spy agency he worked for) for that episode. The island was called "The Village." Number Six tried to escape from the island in various ways but always was returned to his captivity, until in the last episode, which is very difficult to understand (because there is reason to suggest that Number Six was also Number One) he destroys The Village and returns to London and his apartment there. Notice the way The Prisoner asks questions. He wants to gain information about what happened to him and follows up replies by Number Two with other questions. *The Prisoner* was a cult series, and many followers suggested that the pause in the middle of "You are…Number Six" really should be construed to mean "You are Number One."

The conversation between The Prisoner and Number Two was logical given the situation in which The Prisoner found himself. The situations in which we find ourselves generally shape the conversations we have. We may ask: What determines the way we speak with others? Although we may not be aware of them, there are a large number of factors we take into consideration when we speak with others. I will focus on conversations between two people in my discussion of interpersonal communication. We can look upon conversation as being like a game with certain moves and countermoves that are part of the game.

PLEASED TO MEET YOU !!	WHAT DO YOU DO FOR A LIVING ?	HI !!	GOOD MORNING AFTERNOON EVENING	HOW DID THAT HAPPEN ?	DO YOU KNOW — ?
+ 2	− 30	+ 2	+ 12	+ 15	+ 12
WHERE ARE YOU FROM ? + 6					WHY DID HE/SHE SAY THAT ? + 4
AND THEN WHAT HAPPENED ? + 16					YOUR PLACE OR MINE ?? − 50
TELL ME ABOUT YOURSELF ! + 15	WHAZZ UP ?? − 8	WHAT DO YOU THINK OF ! + 4	WHO TOLD YOU THAT ? + 16	HAVE WE MET BEFORE ? + 2	WHY DO YOU THINK THAT ? + 16

The Game of Conversation

There is turn-taking in conversation, and what we say depends, as Bakhtin pointed out, on what was already said and what we anticipate will be said. So conversation is an art. You have to learn how to respond to questions someone asks you and to ask questions to the person with whom you are conversing. People often interrupt one another during conversations, when something pops into their minds and they don't want to forget that something. It takes two to tango, and it takes cooperation between two people to maintain a conversation. Conversations are narratives and, we find, rule-bound. You have to listen attentively to what is being said in a conversation to maintain it.

There are certain pitfalls that can damage or ruin conversations. Sometimes the person with whom you are conversing isn't really listening to what you say; sometimes a person with whom you are conversing monopolizes the conversation and all you can do is listen, while you find yourself unable to get a word in edgewise. Narcissistic conversationalists shift whatever is being talked about to themselves and look upon a conversation not as something with a give and take but as an opportunity to talk about themselves. When I was teaching, early in my career,

I had a colleague who used our conversations as a means of trying to get information about me that he could use against me—what is called "ambushing." He didn't like me and wanted to sabotage my career any way he could. There is also what can be described as non-listening, which takes place when the person with whom we are conversing isn't really listening to what we say. During conversations, people's minds wander, people remember things they need to do, and people can get distracted in countless other ways.

Purpose of Communication

What we want to achieve from our conversations shapes the way we converse. Lasswell's model of communication described in Chapter 1 goes "who says what to whom in what channel with what effect?" Each of these elements in his model plays a role in interpersonal communication. What I describe as the "purpose" is another way of saying "effect." The "what" involves the content of the conversation—the words spoken, but also, as I will discuss later, the nonverbal messages given by the "who" and the "whom." Another way to think of this is that there are generally certain goals we have in mind when we converse with others—such as getting to know them better or getting information from them or telling them something they need to know—and almost everything we say and do is connected to those goals.

The Structure of Conversations

In their book, *Metaphors We Live By*, linguist George Lakoff and philosopher Mark Johnson deal with conversations in a chapter called "The Coherent Structuring of Experience." They offer some basic components of a two-party conversation (1980:78):

Participants:

The participants are of a certain natural kind, namely people. Here they take the role of speakers. The conversation is defined by what the participants do, and the same participants play a role throughout the conversation.

Parts:

The parts consist of a certain kind of natural activity, talking. Each turn at talking is part of the conversation as a whole, and these parts must be put together in a certain fashion for there to be a coherent conversation.

Stages:

Conversations traditionally have a set of initial conditions and then pass through various stages, including at least a beginning, a central part, and an end....

Linear sequence:

The participants' turn at speaking are ordered in a linear sequence, with the general constraint that the speakers alternate.... Without such constrains on linear sequencing of parts, you get a monologue or a jumble of words.

Causation:

The finish of one turn at talking is expected to result in the beginning of the next turn.

Purpose:

Conversations may serve any number of purposes, but all typical conversations share the purpose of maintaining polite social interaction in a reasonably cooperative manner.

Lakoff and Johnson offer us their version of the structure of a typical conversation. What we learn from them and from other theorists of conversations and interpersonal communication is that there are codes of behavior that have to be followed for a successful conversation. When all the energy in a conversation is devoted to attacking and discrediting the ideas of the other person, you have an argument.

Topics of Conversation

Although in principle there are endless topics people can talk about when conversing, in actuality many of them fall into a certain number of topics:

Conversations about facts. Here, people discuss certain "facts," and raise questions about them. (I've noticed in conversations with friends that sometimes when we wonder about something like when Freud was born or what's the capitol of Belarus, we can get this information from "personal assistants" such as Siri, Okay Google, and now Microsoft's Cortana.)

Conversations about ideas. This is a fertile topic for conversations since ideas are intrinsically interesting since they often have relevance to our lives. This kind of conversation often deals with politics and religion, two generally dangerous subjects to talk about with strangers and sometime even with friends, because they can lead to arguments.

Conversations about events—generally about the kind of topics covered in newspapers and news programs on radio and television: wars in various countries, deaths of famous people, scientific discoveries, the stock market, divorces and illnesses of our friends, and so on.

Conversations about popular culture and elite culture texts. Novels, plays, television shows, movies, songs, football games, and so on are common topics of conversations. They also serve the function of revealing something about one's tastes, identities, nationality, and values. Sports are a good topic for conversation since our attachments to certain teams and speculations about the outcome of certain games is relatively innocuous.

Conversations about other people. People are infinitely complex and interesting, and understanding their motives and behaviors is the subject of many conversations. Some of this kind of conversation has the danger of becoming gossip. Recently, my wife and I went to a friend's house for lunch and got into a conversation about a mutual friend that went on for a very long time, in part because we were speculating about what this person's motives were for doing something he planned to do.

Conversations about oneself. People often talk about themselves during conversations, and often exchange information about themselves. Narcissistic conversationalists only seem to be interesting in talking about themselves and monopolize conversations, interrupting or rerouting the conversation when it is not about themselves. You don't really have a conversation with such people; you just listen to them talk about themselves. This quickly becomes tedious and boring, and I must admit I have a sense of dread when the phone rings and my answering machine tells me such a person is calling.

Here are some matters that shape our reactions during conversations (some of which I discuss in detail in Chapter 9, my chapter on visual and nonverbal communication):

Our voice quality. Is our voice soothing or abrasive and harsh? Too soft to hear easily or too loud?

Our posture and body language. Are we unconsciously turning away from or distancing ourselves from the person with whom we are conversing?

Our use of eye contact. Do we maintain eye contact or look away from the person with whom we are talking?

Our facial expressions. How does the person with whom we are conversing react to our facial expressions?

Our sequencing of interactions? Do we respond to openings given to us for comment or let them pass? Do we interrupt all the time?

Our positioning ourselves with others. Do we sit next to (such as at the corner of a table) or opposite from the person with whom we are conversing?

We can see that there are any number of things we do or don't do that play an important role in conversations I deal with body language and facial expression in some detail in Chapter 9 on visual communication.

Demographics

Here we consider such matters as gender, age, race, ethnicity, level of education, and occupation (including socio-economic class)—all of which play a role in the way we converse. We speak differently to more elderly people than we speak to people our own age or to young children. We speak in a high pitch with toddlers and babies and tend to be respectful when talking to the elderly, to the police, to judges, to clergy, to professors, and to doctors.

Context

For example, consider the place where people are speaking, where they find themselves. The kind of conversations we have are different if we meet someone at a party or in a bar, especially if that person is of a different gender, than we have if we meet in a church or synagogue or mosque or at a lecture. We talk to our classmates one way and to our professors a different way, because of the codes of conversational interaction that exist in colleges and universities.

Roles

According to sociologists, in the course of the day a person may play many roles: mother, wife, doctor, shopper, and so on. The roles we are playing help shape the way we speak to others. Dr. Jane Smith speaks one way with patients, another way with checkout clerks in supermarkets, and yet a different way to her husband and her children. There are certain times when a role we take on is connected to certain obligations. For example, if two people go out on a date, each of them assumes an obligation to converse with the other party and carry on a conversation that each will find interesting and hopefully entertaining.

Interpersonal Relationships: Friendships

Interpersonal relationships have many functions. One of the most important of these involves developing friendships. Friendships usually evolve in distinct stages. We meet someone somewhere by chance—at work, at a party, on the internet, at a bar, wherever. This is known as a role-limited interaction because we generally don't disclose very much about ourselves to one another. The next step involves finding out more about each other to see whether we have interests and tastes in common. Usually people become friends with others who are like them in various ways—who are roughly the same age, have the same education, and status. At the next stage, people start disclosing more, of a personal nature, about themselves. If all goes well, the next step is a caring relationship in which two people feel bonds of affection toward one another. After a period of time this leads towards a more stabilized relationship, in which the friends tend to see one another frequently. This stage is characterized by trust and the ability to share intimate matters. Many friendships remain at this stage, but sometimes, for one reason or another, people drift apart and the friendship wanes.

Some friendships are associative and based on chance relationships, like being students in the same class. When a new semester begins, these friendships often wane. Other friendships involve reciprocity—in which each person does something for the other and both gain from the relationship. Usually there are feelings of mutual affection in this kind of relationship. Relationships among friends, politicians, movie stars, and so on are also one of the most common topics for conversation among people, since we are all fascinated by other people's behavior.

Interpersonal Relationships: Romantic Love

Some friendships turn into love affairs. People "fall in love." But what does it mean to fall in love? When we trip over something and are falling, we have no control over ourselves, and this feeling explains what we mean by falling in love. We've lost control of ourselves, and we hope that when we land, we won't get hurt. It also may explain what happens when love affairs don't work out and we "fall out of love." Before we fall in love, when we think about our partner, there is often some speculating about the suitability of the love affair: is our love object similar to us in important ways, is our love object physically attractive, are the positives more important than the negatives?

Like friendships, love relationships also involve certain steps, from becoming aware of a potential love object, making a connection, getting to know one another better, spending a great deal of time together, becoming passionately (and frequently sexually) involved with one another, and falling in love. Now, in the age of social media, many love affairs start on the

The Game
of Love

internet. There are various sites that help people find others like them, such as J-Dates, Christian Mingle, and so on.

Romantic love is a matter that preoccupies our greatest playwrights, novelists, and pop song writers. It is, for most people, their most important relationship. When I was growing up there was a popular song called "All in the Game" which suggested that love is a game. Seeing love as a game casts it in a much different light than seeing love as something serious and important. If love is a game, if you get tired of playing it with someone, you can stop and find someone else to play the game with. The high rate of divorce in America and many other countries suggests that love is one of the more difficult relationships to maintain. And that is because in all relationships there are inevitably conflicts that arise that have to be resolved one way or another. If there are too many conflicts and they become too serious, romantic love isn't enough to hold people together, and they separate or get divorced. A great deal of popular music is devoted to problems with love affairs, with being cheated on, with being "dumped," and other complications leading to heartbreak and sadness.

Interpersonal Relationships: The Family

The family is the primary relationship for the first two decades of our lives—or was before the boomerang generation moved back home—but the definition of the family has changed a great deal over the years. There are now many one-parent families and many couples living together who are not married. And there are large numbers of people who are living alone, some of whom may have been previously married. It is from our families that we learn the codes of conduct that shape our behavior. I dealt with that in my discussion in Chapter 4 of Clotaire Rapaille's *The Culture Code*. He used the term "imprinting" for describing what happens during the first seven years of a child's life.

Raising children can be very stressful, and many studies have found that families are happiest when they enter the "empty nest" stage and the married or unmarried partners have only one another to deal with. They can forget about sibling rivalry, adolescent traumas of one sort or another ("I got dumped" or "I totaled your car"), and the difficulties of maintaining harmony in a family in which children may not like one another and there is bickering and other displays of hostility. Not all families in America are full of conflict, of course. In most families here there's a certain amount of conflict but it can be managed tolerably well.

There is also the matter of cultural diversity. In many cultures, where individualism is not as pronounced as in America, families are all-important and children and their parents and other relatives maintain very strong ties to one another all through their lives. This kind of arrangement generally can be found in traditional societies or in American families made up of people from other countries. As I explain next, different cultural backgrounds mean different cultural codes, which affect interpersonal relationships in profound ways.

Cultural Codes and Cultural Backgrounds

Our nationalities and their cultural codes have an impact on our speech. Americans tend to be friendly when they meet stranger, while people from some countries, such as Japan, are more reserved. People with similar racial, religious, national, and ethnic backgrounds often find it easier to converse with one another, because they have so many shared values and beliefs, than people who are different from one another in these respects. (See Chapter 4)

There are certain rules of conversational etiquette that conversationalists should follow, such as not to interrupt others while they are speaking, not to embarrass others, and not to speak in too loud a voice. That is, there are certain conventions that people are supposed to follow when having a conversation, but these conventions vary from situation to situation.

Conversational Skills

As I've pointed out many times in this book, our conversational skills play a major role in interpersonal communication. Some people who have not learned how to carry on a conversation are difficult to talk with, while other people, who know how to converse with others, are easy to talk with. I deal with the complexities of conversation and the rules for carrying on a conversation in my discussion of the work of Labov and Waletzky on narratives—for conversations are, in essence, narratives—and the work of Bakhtin, on intertextuality and conversation. What many people do is develop a repertoire of topics on which they can converse with relative ease, such as movies they've seen, singers they like, sports teams they follow, skills and interests they have, places they've been, and so on.

Selective Attention, Inattention, and Disclosure

Psychologists tell us that we are generally **selective** in our communication, neglecting to reply to certain things, not paying attention at times to threads in a conversation, and being careful to provide only certain information to others. This process of selective disclosure makes sense since we don't want to take any chance of alienating people we've just met or even ones we've known for a long time. For example, when I went to college in the fifties, gay men hid their sexual orientation from others—except those they knew as gay—because of social pressures. I belong to a group of people who read short stories and discuss them once a week. This group has been meeting for years, yet though everyone in the group has known one another for a long time, it is only over time that members of the group reveal certain things about themselves.

Personality Factors

Carl Jung, probably the most famous psychologist after Freud, wrote a book, *Personality Types*, that stimulated interest in the subject. Two American psychologists, Katherine Briggs and her daughter Isabel Briggs Myers, have done research on personality and claim that there are sixteen different personality types. They suggest that these personality types found in people help explain their behavior. Thus, people who are shy, who are "inner directed" or "introverted," probably find it more difficult to converse with strangers than do outgoing, "extroverted," "outer directed" individuals, who enjoy conversing with most everyone. Narcissists, who are obsessed with themselves, are more likely to talk about their activities and interests in conversations than are shy people, who tend to avoid talking about themselves—or even conversing with others.

Channel or Mode of Communication

We can consider text messages between two people as interpersonal (but not face-to-face) communication. Some people send hundreds of texts a day to their friends, who reply to these texts, thus creating interpersonal communication. Generally, these texts are rather short without much content, which has led some scholars to describe them as "**phatic**" communication, a term coined by Polish anthropologist Bronislaw Malinowski to describe communication that is little more than noise to indicate sociability rather than to impart information.

In my discussion of focal points in mass communication in Chapter 1 I listed five focal points that can also be used to understand interpersonal communication:

Focal Point	Interpersonal Communication
Artist	Speaker
Audience	Listener—Recipient of communication
Medium	Human voice or internet for texting
Art	What a speaker says
America	The context in which the conversation is held

This analysis suggests that a conversation can be looked upon as being like a work of art created by two performance artists, and though conversations are seemingly casual, we recognize that a great deal of thinking and effort goes into holding a good conversation. In this model, the "art" stands for the messages that are exchanged between the two conversationalists. If the conversation is being held in America, we must recognize, also, that there are many American cultural conversational and behavioral codes that play a role in the way we converse—even though we may not be aware of these rules and codes. In **egalitarian** countries like America, people speak to one another as equals (even though we may not actually be equals), but in hierarchical societies, such as England, one's status and the status of the person being talked to plays a much bigger role.

Summary

In this chapter I've dealt with a number of matters relating to interpersonal communication, which is conventionally defined as communication between two persons. I've examined the nature, purposes, and structure of conversations, the role of demographics and context in interpersonal relationships, and topics such as friendship, romantic love, and the family. I've also discussed the role that cultural codes in the United States and other countries play in interpersonal relationships. One thing we learn from this chapter is that there are many unrecognized rules that affect our interpersonal relationships and behavior in general.

Applications

1. How do cultural codes affect the way we converse with others? Give an example of a conversation you had recently.

2. Correlate topics of conversation with age. What gets discussed in each age group?

    a. Toddlers

    b. Teenagers

    c. Middle-Age people

    d. The Elderly

3. Write a short dialogue in which a French man, an English man, and an Italian woman converse using stereotyped national characteristic to shape the dialogue.

4. Listen to several of your friends and try to identify specific conversational habits that are unique to them. Can you link any of them to a specific nationality, age, class, gender, or ethnicity?

5. When you talk to a computer chip and it answers your questions, are you having a conversation? If so, how do you justify your position? If not, why not?

6. Examine the lyrics of some romantic songs. How is love communicated by the writers? What metaphors do you find? How do the writers of the songs characterize romantic love? What do the songs reveal about romantic love?

Chapter 6

Communicating in Groups

Messages: An Introduction to Communication by Arthur Asa Berger, 118–135.

For Baudrillard, contemporary society is a postmodern society which is no longer structured by production in which the individual conforms to its needs but by symbolic exchange. It is a heterogeneous society of different groups with their own codes and practices of everyday life at the level of discourse, lifestyles, bodies, sexuality, communication, etc., and it involves the rejection of the logic of production and its instrumental rationality that dominated the modernist society of capitalism. Capitalism now has been replaced by a consumer society which is characterized by a proliferation of signs, the media and messages, environmental design, cybernetic steering systems, contemporary art and a sign culture. It is a society of simulations based on the new forms of technology and culture.... A world of hyper-reality is created in which everything in the world is simulated in the sense that models created by images replace the real.

David F. Walsh, "Subject/Object"

If we want groups to serve as incubators for conscious messages...we have to keep groups below the 150 Tipping point. Above that point, there begin to be structural impediments to the ability of a group to agree and act with one voice. If we want to, say, develop schools in disadvantaged communities that can successfully counteract the poisonous atmosphere of their surrounding neighborhoods, this tells us what we're probably better off building lots of little schools than one or two big ones. The Rule of 150 says that congregants of a rapidly expanding church, or the members of a social club, or anyone in a group banking on the epidemic spread of shared ideals needs to be particularly cognizant of the perils of bigness. Crossing the 150 line is a small change than can make a big difference.

Malcolm Gladwell, *The Tipping Point: How Little Things Can Make a Big Difference*

In this chapter I explain how I interpret the term "group," discuss **grid-group theory** and its relation to the media, offer a case study of small group to which I belong, and say something about the roles played by members of various kinds of groups. As the quote about Baudrillard makes clear, modern society is composed of a multitude of different kinds of groups, and these groups are characterized by the variety of different interests and kinds of messages they send and receive, in a society that is now shaped by consumer cultures and simulations, leading to what he described as a hyper-reality. Baudrillard has argued, perhaps facetiously, that Disneyland is the real America and America is a simulation of Disneyland. The main point is that groups play an all-important role in our lives, and how we communicate in groups is a fascinating topic. And Malcolm Gladwell points out that the size of our groups makes a great deal of difference and that when a group becomes larger than 150 members, it becomes much more difficult for it to function efficiently. I also discuss "groupthink" and conclude with a discussion of **organizational communication**.

Defining Groups

When I told my wife that I would be writing about groups, the first thing she asked was, "How do you define a group? How many people are there in a group?" If you're going to write about groups, it is reasonable that you have a good idea of what a group is and how many people make a group. We don't talk about two people being a group, so, at the very least, it is fair to assume that groups have more than two people in them. Conventionally, we understand small groups to have between three to twelve people and assume that more than twelve people makes a medium size group and approximately a hundred and fifty or more people a large group. Saying that small groups have between three and twelve people is, of course, quite arbitrary. It doesn't make sense to say that if a thirteenth person joins a small group it is now a medium size group but we have to draw the line somewhere and generally speaking, communications theorists suggest that small groups contain no more than twelve people.

I will define a small group, for our purposes, as a long-lasting collection of between three and twelve individuals who interact with one another, share certain behavioral codes and purposes, are interdependent, and have something in common. We can distinguish between groups and teams. Teams are small groups in which everyone's role is clearly defined and that generally focus on some task. It is this task that shapes most of their communication.

What groups have in common may be tied to matters like their race, their religion, their occupations, their gender, their age, their interests, their hobbies, and so on. When I first moved to Mill Valley, a small town in Marin County, California, I saw a sign at a supermarket which said a group of people with small printing presses was being formed. I had studied small press printing at the University of Iowa, so I went to the first meeting, and that meeting led to the formation of what we called "The Small Press Club of Marin County." That club had meetings once a month and lasted for a dozen years.

A good way to deal with this matter of the size needed to form a group is to use a classification system devised by one of America's most important sociologists, Charles H. Cooley. He said there were two kinds of groups: *primary* groups, such as the family, in which there is face-to-face communication and where children learn norms and rules, and *secondary* groups, such as those based on socio-economic class or ethnicity, which are not based on face-to-face communication and which are, like small groups, categories of people based on something they share in common. I will say something about large groups and then deal with small groups. I begin with groupthink and the groups that are generated by its opposite, **postmodernism**.

Groupthink and Postmodernism

I begin with an explanation of "groupthink" and with a discussion of how groupthink shapes our perceptions of the world. Small groups, like families, have the **power** to shape people's perceptions and the way they communicate with one another. Clotaire Rapaille's work on imprinting shows the power of the family and the national culture, and Basil Bernstein's work on codes showed there was a relationship between social class and the way children learn to speak. A psychologist, Irving L. Janis, wrote a book titled *Groupthink: Psychological Studies of Policy*

Decisions and Fiascos. He argues that in some groups, the need for conformity is so powerful (what he calls "groupthink) that it hinders the ability of the group to respond to challenges in the best possible way.

Gustav Le Bon

If you take groupthink and enlarge it to deal with much larger groups of people, you get **crowds**, the subject of the French sociologist Gustave Le Bon's famous book, *The Crowd*. In his book, first published in 1895, Le Bon described the characteristics of crowds (1960:13–14):

> Under certain given circumstances, and only under those circumstances, an agglomeration of men presents new characteristics very different from those of the individuals composing it. The sentiments and ideas of all the persons in the gathering take one and the same direction, and their conscious personality vanishes. A collective mind is formed, doubtless transitory, but presenting very clearly defined characteristics.

We know the power of crowds gathered in public spaces. It was crowds that led to the overthrow of a dictator in Tunisia and then to what we describe as the Arab spring, and it was crowds in Kiev that led to the overthrow of the president in Ukraine. Crowds matter, and now, thanks to Twitter, they can be formed very quickly for political action. What Janis called groupthink can be seen as similar, in nature, to the mindset found in the "collective mind" in crowds. And crowds do not always behave in rational and non-violent ways.

David Walsh, in the quotation at the beginning of this chapter, argues that postmodernism, the kind of society that many culture theorists believe we live in now, is characterized by hyper-individualism and a heterogeneous collection of groups that live, more or less, by their own rules. A French scholar, Jean François Lyotard, described postmodernism as "incredulity toward metanarratives," by which he meant that in postmodern society, the old narratives and stories that guided us in the periods before postmodernism (including **modernism**) were abandoned. This led to a loss of faith in reason and of a belief in universal values like striving for truth and the notion that there were **ethical** absolutes. All of this affects the way we think and speak.

These "metanarratives" anchored our belief in progress, and when they disappeared, everyone was left to his or her own devices in randomly organized groups, each with its own rules. This led to an ongoing crisis of legitimacy. Can we ever ask, "What is the right thing to do?" or are questions like that irrelevant in postmodern societies where, with no widely accepted metanarratives to guide us, "anything goes."

Aaron Wildavsky

Grid-Group Theory

Some social scientists, known as grid-group theorists, believe that we all belong to one of four lifestyle groups which shape our thinking and behavior. This approach to understanding groups, what is known as grid-group theory, posits that in all societies, there are four "lifestyles" that shape our politics, consumer choices, and other aspects of our behavior. Aaron Wildavsky, a political scientist who taught at the University of California at Berkeley for many years, explained that these lifestyles are based on whether there are few or many rules for the group (grid) and the strength or weakness of their group's boundaries (group). These lifestyles are:

Lifestyle	Group Boundaries	Rules and Prescriptions
Individualists	Weak	Few
Fatalists	Weak	Numerous
Elitists	Strong	Numerous
Egalitarians	Strong	Few

Wildavsky described what the groups are like—what we can call **political cultures** or "lifestyles" for the non-political aspects of these groups—and how they are formed:

Strong groups with numerous prescriptions that vary with social roles combine to form hierarchical collectivism [**elitists**]. Strong groups whose members follow few prescriptions form an egalitarian culture, a shared life of voluntary consent, without coercion or inequality. Competitive individualism joins few prescriptions with weak boundaries, thereby encouraging ever new combinations. When groups are weak and prescriptions are strong, so that decisions are made for them by people on the outside, the controlled culture is fatalistic. (quoted in Berger 1989:6)

If Wildavsky and the other grid-group theorists are correct, everyone in modern societies, whether they realize it or not, belongs to one of these four lifestyles, and their behavior is shaped by this membership.

Mary Douglas, the English social-anthropologist who developed grid-group theory, offered an example of the role these groups play in our lives. She writes, in an essay, "In Defence of Shopping" (1997:17–18):

We have to make a radical shift away from thinking about consumption as a manifestation of individual choice. Culture itself is the result of myriads of individual choices, not primarily between commodities but between kinds of relationships. The basic choice that a rational individual has to make is the choice about what kind of society to live in. According to that choice, the rest follows. Artefacts are selected to demonstrate that choice. Food is eaten, clothes are worn, cinema, books, music, holidays, all the rest are choices that conform with the initial choice for a form of society.

Douglas is using the word "society" for "lifestyle." Her point is that the group we belong to, namely the lifestyle we choose to belong to—even though we may not be conscious that we have chosen a lifestyle—affects our behavior, and, of course, by implication, the way we communicate with others.

Members of these lifestyles may not be aware that they "belong" to their lifestyle, but their lifestyle shapes their political choices, what they consume, what they talk about, and how they talk about things. They are also antagonistic to other lifestyles. The value of grid-group theory is that it limits the number of groups that are important to us to four. Of course, within these lifestyles are other groups, clubs, and associations—small groups—that reinforce the values of the overarching lifestyle. We can suggest that our lifestyles shape not only the things we buy but also what we talk about and the way we talk about things and, thus, the kind of "speech" we use and the media to which we are attracted.

Groups and Cultural Choices

Let me offer an example of the way our lifestyles shape our choice of popular culture in the chart that follows. In a class I taught on popular culture and media, I explained grid-group theory and had my students read material by Wildavsky and Douglas and others and then use grid-group theory to determine what texts people in each lifestyle would probably like:

Pop Culture	Individualist	Elitist	Egalitarian	Fatalist
Songs	My Way	God Save the Queen	We Are the World	Anarchy in the UK
Books	Looking Out for Number One	The Prince	I'm Okay, You're Okay	1984
Games	Monopoly	Chess	New Games	Russian Roulette

Logically speaking, **Individualists** would be expected to like songs such as "I Did It My Way," while Elitists would prefer songs that respect hierarchy, such as "God Save the Queen," and Egalitarians would like "We Are the World," while **Fatalists** might prefer "Anarchy in the UK." An Elitist game is chess (with its kings, queens, pawns, and so forth), an Individualist game is Monopoly (which is about making money), an Egalitarian game might be a "new game" like Frisbee (with no score keeping and no winners or losers), and the quintessential Fatalist game would be Russian Roulette. We can look at other kinds of media and popular culture and see how members of the four lifestyles would choose certain television programs to watch, magazines to read, and so on. We can think of these lifestyles as large diffuse social groupings that hover in the background and play a role in the small groups we join, the kind of media we watch, and the way we communicate with others. What people watch on television and films they've seen are important topics of conversation with many people whose popular culture/

media preferences tend to be different for each of the four life-styles, as I've shown above.

Roles Played by Members of Small Groups

If interpersonal communication is complex, small group communication is even more complicated, because generally there are more people involved in the communication process and in negotiating with one another. I've defined groups and said something about the size of small groups. There are many other factors to consider in dealing with small groups and the communication processes that take place inside them.

There are many roles that members of small groups play. Below I list some of them as they apply to a small group to which I belong. There are twelve members in this group. We read short stories and talk about them, and then we discuss some topic, chosen by the host, while we sit around a table and have fruit, coffee and cake. One example of a discussion topic was "If you could pass any law through Congress, what would it be?" The topics often are about current events, politics, news stories, and that kind of thing. With this description of the short story group in mind, let's consider the roles that various members of the group play—sometimes a member of the group plays more than one role, I should add.

Information Seekers

They offer or seek facts, give opinions and seek for clarifications on issues being discussed relative to the story or the discussion question.

New Idea Contributors

They provide new ideas or new perspectives on characters and events in the stories, bringing in information from other sources, such as their background as psychologists and therapists.

Enhancers

They explain what events in the story mean and expand upon the social and cultural significance of the story. They do the same for discussion questions.

Judges

They give their opinions about the quality of the stories and events and characters in the stories. They also critique the topics under discussion and comments made during the discussion.

Recording Secretaries

They do the scheduling and take care of things in general.

Dominators and Dominatrices

They tend to monopolize the discussions and have something to say about everything. They tend to be impulsive and fast on the draw.

Drama Queens and Drama Kings

They turn discussions of the stories into long and dramatic recitals of (exciting to them) events that have happened to them at some time in their lives. The stories often serve as a means of their becoming very emotional.

Passive Aquiesants and Shrinking Violets

They remain silent unless asked to comment on a story or the discussion topic. They have to coaxed to contribute to the discussion.

My wife and I have belonged to this group of twelve people for more than thirty years. The group is made up of five couples and two wives whose husbands don't attend meetings. The members of our group are all elderly retired professional people whose "lifestyle" I would describe as egalitarian. The members of the group are all well-educated, with everyone having a college education. Eight members of the group have advanced degrees and four have doctorates. All of the members of the group are in the upper-middle class and above. Many of the members belong to other groups, such as book reading groups, film groups, philosophy study groups, and political action groups. As might be expected, over the years members of the group have come and gone, but the present configuration of the group has been the same for around ten years. Each month we meet in one of the members' homes, and we collectively work out a schedule for when we will meet each month.

My role with the group is to find collections of short stories for the group to read, but the group makes a final decision collectively about which books to read. I also keep the calendar, which involves noting down which family will host the group and which month they will do so. I send announcements to the members about which story we are reading and where we will be meeting. The inter-group dynamics are interesting. We have one member who has a great deal to say about everything and would completely take over our discussions if left to his own devices. I would describe him as a dominator. Keeping him under control is a constant problem. We have another member, who I would describe as a drama queen, who used to seize control of the discussions to talk about her experiences and various traumas, the darling things her grandchildren had to say and that kind of thing, sometimes for ten or fifteen minutes. I was able to convince her to stop that kind of behavior. Then we have a woman who tends to be shy in groups and has to be coaxed to say anything, though usually what she has to say is quite interesting. She is a shrinking violet. Other members vary between contributing to the discussion from time to time to just listening to the discussions. One member generally says nothing. He is a passive acquiesant in my typology.

My task, as the person who organizes the meetings and more or less keeps the group going, is to try to encourage the shy members and restrain the talkative ones, to prevent the drama queen from taking control of the discussions, and to find a way to have everyone participate. Having been a professor for forty years and taught many seminars, I have a lot of experience at this kind of thing. What we've learned to do over the years is find ways of negotiating with one another so there is relative harmony in the group. The only rule we have is to not interrupt others while they are speaking, but that rule is difficult to sustain.

Organizational Structure of Small Groups

Communication scholars make distinctions between high context and low context cultures and the groups that form under each kind of culture. This distinction between groups was first formulated by anthropologist Edward T. Hall, who suggested that in high context cultures, it is the cultural norms and shared beliefs that shape conversation, while in low context cultures, people have to be very clear and explicit in verbal messages about what they believe. Cohesion is an important aspect of some small groups which often develop certain norms. These norms vary from culture to culture. Thus, in the United States being punctual is considered important, while in other countries being "late" is the norm and people don't expect others to be punctual.

In some groups, the interaction patterns are centralized and communication is controlled by the group leader or leaders, while in other groups, there are no leaders and group communication is decentralized. Groups also vary in their formats. In my short story group, we all sit around in a circle in a "roundtable" format and there's no pattern about who speaks and when they speak. But some groups are much more formal and may have panels of members who sit in front of the other members of the group and have a set pattern that shapes when they speak.

Groups also vary in terms of the kinds of communication found in them. Thus, some communication involves scheduling and procedures, while other communication focuses on goals of the group or tasks they have to discuss. It is not unusual for there to be what can be called "chit-chat" in which people chat about things of interest. This kind of communication establishes harmony among the members of the group and builds a positive sense of the value of the group—contributing to group cohesion.

Groups can have three kinds of organization. There can be a hierarchical leaders and followers group organization, there can be revolving or circulating leadership groups (with rules for who leads for how long, how leaders are chosen, and when), and there can be leaderless groups with nobody in charge—but maintained by procedural technicians. Nobody in the short story reading group has the power to make anyone do anything; everything is done by voluntary consent, so we are a leaderless group. That is possible—though not easy—in small groups but not practical in larger ones, and impossible in groups larger than 150 members, as Malcolm Gladwell explains.

Small groups are important because they help us counter the stresses created by alienating mass societies, where we are relatively anonymous. In groups, we find friends (and sometimes enemies), we find things to do, we learn things, we accomplish things, and we often have long term face-to-face relationships that help us establish our identities and that enhance our sense of self. I recall asking my students, a number of years ago, about the groups in their high schools and discovering that there were more than a dozen groups in typical California high schools, such as "preppies," "cheerleaders," "jocks," "skaters," "white punks on dope," and so on.

Organizational Communication

Many Americans belong to small groups such as the short story reading group to which I belong. America is famous for having had many voluntary organizations that people belonged to—everything from service organizations like the Rotary Club and Boy Scouts to sports teams, political clubs, and religious organizations. This membership in voluntary associations has waned in recent years. We often belong to or work for a number of larger groups and organizations. One of the most important aspects of group communication involves organizations. The larger the organization is, the more complex it is and the more structured and formalized are its channels of communication.

We can define an organization as an entity made up of people who share a collective goal, purpose, and culture. Some typical organizations are businesses, universities, and governmental agencies. Let us take major universities as our example. Universities are complex institutions whose primary missions are to teach students and conduct research. In large and complex institutions, there are usually formal and informal channels through which messages move. In formal channels, some messages move from the top (the president and the administration) down (to the faculty and students), some messages move up (from students and the faculty up to the administration and the president), and some move horizontally (from professors to other professors or administrators to other administrators or students to other students).

Because they have to deal with many thousands of people, educational institutions develop bureaucratic structures, with formal rules and procedures, generally decided upon by the administration and the faculty. Organizations tend to be hierarchical, with members having different statuses and powers. In most complex organizations there are chains of communication to be followed. Universities, like many complex organizations, are run by committees. In any academic department there are usually many committees that deal with everything from curriculum to hiring, retention, and tenure, and sometimes many subcommittees as well. The administration in universities has to deal with a number of things—everything from parking, the construction of new buildings, student health, and student organizations to security.

What I have sketched out is an example of formal communication using officially approved pathways. Informal organization communications don't use officially designated pathways but involve communication between members of the organization who meet at coffee breaks, lunches, when they happen to bump into one another, and that kind of thing. This is sometimes known as "the grapevine," which can be described as information that flows in organizations and whose authorship is frequently unknown.

Organizations develop distinctive cultures, which can be described as ways of thinking and behaving that are shared by people in the organization. As a rule of thumb we may say that wherever you find groups of people together for substantial periods of time, which is what you find with organizations, certain rituals become important and distinctive "corporate cultures" that reflect the corporation's identity are created. Because organizations play such an important role in our lives, there is a vast literature on them and on organizational communication. There are more than 250,000 books on organizations and around 3,000 books on organizational communication at Amazon.com.

Political Parties

In my discussion of grid-group theory, I dealt with "lifestyles," which, when applied to politics, can be described as political cultures. Aaron Wildavsky was interested in grid-group theory because he could use it to understand political cultures. These four political cultures, let us recall, are individualists, elitists, egalitarians, and fatalists. These political cultures shape our thinking about politics and our voting and, for many people, much of their conversations—especially when there are elections. Before the development of social media, most political messaging took the form of advertisements on radio and television, printed fliers, and newspaper advertisements. That changed with the development of social media.

Now political parties use social media, targeted to individuals and groups, to spread their messages and to get money for campaigns. My wife and I happen to be Democrats. It is not an exaggeration to say that in recent weeks I have received at least five emails a day asking for money—generally five dollars and up—from someone of importance in the Democratic Party like Nancy Pelosi or Vice President Joe Biden. An example of one of these emails (from dccc.org) follows. It deals with a decision of the Supreme Court that companies run by persons with certain religious beliefs do not need to provide contraception materials to workers in these companies.

BREAKING: Republicans in Congress block birth control bill

We are fuming:

First: The conservative men on the Supreme Court made the disastrous Hobby Lobby decision.

Then: Today, Republicans rejected a bill that would have overturned Hobby Lobby and restored women's access to cost-free contraception.

Now: Republicans are doubling down on their war on women with a hollow birth control bill that does absolutely nothing for working women. It simply allows women to purchase their own birth control out of pocket—which they can already do at a huge cost. It's a slimy attempt to fool people into thinking that they care. It's offensive.

We refuse to let them get away with this.

The only way we can put an end to this war on women madness is by kicking these jokers out of Washington. To do that, you need to step up and show your support. Are you in?

These emails are all persuasive messages that use emotional arguments to obtain donations of money for political advertising to support Democratic candidates. The partisan nature of the communication shows how the sender understands the message is going to an audience that agrees with the sender. Aristotle would say these messages use **ethos** (the messages are often from important political figures like the vice president), **pathos** (emotional arguments found in language such as "war on women madness" and "slimy attempt"), and logos (the argument made about women's rights). We find the same combination of emotion and arguments from important political figures in political speeches of candidates from all political parties.

The messages I receive focus on issues that most Democrats feel are important, such as women's rights to free contraception,

which is a provision of Obamacare, or immigration reform. Americans are now flooded with emails in an attempt to get people to vote for candidates from the different political parties. The cost of the 2012 campaigns for congress and the presidency was more than six billion dollars, and it will be in the billions for the 2014 congressional campaigns.

Summary

This chapter has dealt with communication in groups, ranging from small groups (at least three people) and small social groups people belong to, such as my short-story reading group, to large groups like those found working in corporations, organizations, and institutions, such as universities, often with many thousands of employees. Central to the analysis of group communication is the notion that the messages we send are supposed to follow certain codes and rules which are based on the interests of the receivers of our messages and the nature of the group involved in the communication. Political communication we find has been affected by the growth of social media and is changing from complete reliance on radio and television advertising to targeting specific individuals and groups who are members of the various political parties using social media as described in the solicitation in this chapter.

Applications

1. What is the role of crowds in politics? Give a contemporary example of crowd behavior in the news and analyze its role.

2. Which lifestyle do you belong to: individualist, egalitarian, elitist, or fatalist? Why do you think you belong to it? One way to find the answer to this question is by filling out the chart below. If all your choices end up in one column, you probably are a member of that lifestyle.

3. Analyze a television situation comedy that revolves around a small group. What dynamics that you've learned about can you see in the group? What roles do the various characters play?

4. Is watching sitcoms a way of participating (vicariously) in small groups? Explain your answer.

5. Use the typology of kinds of people who are members of small groups to analyze some group to which you belong. Are there certain kinds of people whose behavior isn't covered by the typology? Describe them and the role they play in your group.

Pop Culture	Individualist	Elitist	Egalitarian	Fatalist
Films				
Television shows				
Magazines				
Heroes				
Heroines				

Chapter 7

Mass Media

Messages: An Introduction to Communication by Arthur Asa Berger, 136–157.

With media and culture playing such important roles in contemporary life, it is obvious that we must come to understand our cultural environment if we want control over our lives. Yet there are many approaches to the study of media, culture, and society in separate disciplines and academic fields.... We would advocate the usefulness of a wide range of theoretical and methodological approaches to the study of media, culture, and society, yet we do not believe that any one theory or method is adequate to engage the richness, complexity, variety, and novelty displayed in contemporary constellations of rapidly proliferating cultural forms and new media.

Meenakshi Gigi Durham and Douglas M. Kellner, eds.
Media and Cultural Studies: KeyWorks

The study of mass communication is based on the premise that the media have significant effects, yet there is little agreement on the nature and extent of these assumed effects. This uncertainty is the more surprising since everyday experience provides countless, if minor, examples of influence. We dress for the weather as forecast, buy something because of an advertisement, go to a film mentioned in a newspaper, react in countless ways to media news, to films, to music on the radio, and so on. There are many reported cases of negative media publicity concerning, for instance, food contamination or adulteration, leading to significant changes in food consumption behaviour.

Denis McQuail, *Mass Communication Theory: An Introduction,* 3rd Edition

We use the term "mass media" to deal with communication between a relatively small number of people, who create and perform the texts carried by the mass media, and large numbers of people—the audiences—who receive the mass mediated communication. With the development of the internet, things have changed considerably, and now individuals can communicate with large numbers of people through blogs and comments on social media, such as Facebook or Twitter. It is possible for someone to have hundreds or even thousands or hundreds of thousands of "friends" or "followers" who receive his or her messages on blogs, tweets on Twitter, and postings on Facebook. I have several hundred "friends" on Facebook, most of whom I've never met. It is useful to see how the media have developed over the years with the timeline that follows. I begin this discussion of media with a timeline showing the development of mass media and social media sites. Then I offer statistics on media use in the United States. Next I discuss kinds of **violence**, **mass mediated violence**, and the related topic of media ethics. Finally, I offer a summary of some of the more important theories of mass-mediated communication.

Timeline for Development of Media

1833   Mass Circulation Newspapers

1876   Telephone

1895   Silent Films

1926   First Radio Network

1927   First Sound Film

1931   Television invented

1933   FM Radio

1962   First Communications Satellite

1969   Internet

1972   First Video Game: Pong

1975   Personal Computer

1978   Cellular Phone Service

1981   Music Television

1989   World Wide Web

1995   **Digital** Cell Phones

1996   Google

2001   MP3 Technology

2002   Satellite, Web-Based Radio and Television

2004   Facebook

2006   Twitter

2009   Four Square

2010   Instagram, Pinterest

2011   Snapchat, Google+

Media Usage in the United States

This timeline shows that the development of new technologies and modifications of older media technologies in recent years have led to the creation of digital devices that have played an increasingly important role in our daily lives and, in particular, in shaping our time use. The statistics below are taken from a Mashable site (mashable.com/2014/03/05/american-digital -media-hours/), but the table is my construction. Time the average person spends daily:

05:02	Television	00:32	Time Shifted TV
02:46	Radio	00:12	Game Console
01:07	Smartphone	00:09	DVD/Blu Ray
01:01	Internet on PC	00:02	Multimedia Device

The average person in the United States, as the statistics above indicate, watches more than five hours of television, listens to the radio for more than two hours, and spends around an hour with cell phones every day. Other countries may show similar statistics on media usage. It is also estimated that the average American spends eight hours a day looking at screens of one kind or another, such as computer monitors, mobile phone screens, tablet screens, television screens, and film screens.

Time Spent Per Day with Media by Adults and Teenagers

Other statistics from other research companies have slightly different figures from the Mashable/Statistica site discussed above. Census statistics indicate that in 2010, adults in the United States spent almost eleven hours a day with media and in 2013, close to an additional hour per day consuming media. The media statistics on children and teens are even more dramatic. The Kaiser Family Foundation's survey on "Media Use Over Time Among all 8- to 18-year-olds" taken in 2010 (www.kff.org/entmedia/upload/8010.pdf) offers some remarkable data:

> Five years ago, we reported that young people spent an average of nearly 6½ hours (6:21) a day with media—and managed to pack more than 8½ hours (8:33) worth of media content into that time by multitasking. At that point it seemed that young people's lives were filled to the bursting point with media. Today, however, those levels of use have been shattered.
>
> Over the past five years, young people have increased the amount of time they spend consuming media by an hour and seventeen minutes daily, from 6:21 to 7:38—almost the amount of time most adults spend at work each day, except that young people use media seven days a week instead of five.

Moreover, given the amount of time they spend using more than one medium at a time, today's youth pack a total of 10 hours and 45 minutes worth of media content into those daily 7½ hours—an increase of almost 2¼ hours of media exposure per day over the past five years.

If both young people and adults spend that much time each day with the media, the question naturally arises: What effects does all this involvement with the media have on us as individuals and on society? That was a question raised by Harold Lasswell in his model of communication described in the first chapter. He asked, "Who says what to whom in what channel with what effects?"

There is a debate among media critics about the impact of the mass media upon individuals and society. Some critics suggest that the media now bring us the arts and information that refine us culturally and enhance our understanding of politics and other aspects of society. They argue, also, that our exposure to the violence that permeates the mass media is not harmful because it acts as a **catharsis**. Thus, the effect of exposure to media violence does not lead individuals to become violent but diffuses their anger and purges them of it. We can call them "catharsis" critics. The term originated in the writings of Aristotle.

Those on the opposite side of the fence argue that the impact of media is much more powerful and longer lasting than the catharsis critics believe, and while social scientists haven't been able to prove that there's a connection between exposure to violence and violent behavior, there is often a correlation that should make us be concerned. There is a kind of contagion effect in which some disturbed individuals, who are exposed to violence on television and in films, are led to imitate it. Thus, in the United States, in recent years there have been a series of mass murders—the most terrible being the killing of twenty elementary school children and six adults in Sandy Hook by a disturbed twenty year old man, Adam Lanza, on December 14, 2012. This followed shortly after another mass killing a while earlier in the United States. Lanza was a big fan of violent video games, though we cannot assume that it was the video games that drove him to kill all the people he did, including his mother. *USA Today* reports (www.usatoday.com/story/news/ nation/2013/09/16/mass-killings-data) that since 2006 there have been more than 200 mass killings (defined as a killing with four or more victims, not including the killer) in America, at a rate of approximately one every two weeks.

Media and Kinds of Violence

Our attitudes towards violence in the media are shaped to a considerable degree by the kind of violence we are considering; as we can see from this chart, there are many different kinds of violence found in the media. I deal with this topic in terms of polar oppositions.

Kinds of Violence: Polar Oppositions

mediated violence	violence we see directly
comic violence	serious violence
intentional violence	accidental violence
violence to individuals	violence to groups
police violence (just)	criminal violence
verbal violence	physical violence
"fake" violence (pro wrestling)	"true" violence (bar brawl)
violence against heroes	violence against villains
violence against women	violence against men

This table shows that there are many kinds of violence and that it is not possible to make generalizations about violence without taking the various topics in the table into account. Do we feel the same way about violence committed by someone who is insane and someone who is sane?

There is also a debate about whether exposure to violence leads to a catharsis and a relaxation of tension, as Aristotelians believe, or leads to more violence from people who see it in the media, as many social scientists believe. There is also the matter of the kind of violence found in mass mediated texts. For example, in some television shows and films, there can be a considerable amount of "weak" violence and one event of what we might call "serious" violence that shapes our emotional response to the text. We may be exposed to "fake" violence when watching professional wrestling matches (which we now recognize as being a kind of theater), but this "fake" violence still can generate strong emotions in the people watching the matches live in the areas where they take place and in television audiences. Our position on media violence depends, to a certain degree, on our beliefs about the nature of art and its functions in society.

Let me offer, now, two opposing positions on media violence. The first is on "The Effects of Media Violence on Society" by Craig Anderson and Brad Bushman (2002:2377–2379):

Concerns about the negative effects of prolonged exposure to violent television programming emerged shortly after broadcasting began in 1946. By 1972 sufficient empirical evidence had accumulated for the U.S. Surgeon General to comment that "...televised violence, indeed, does have an adverse effect on certain members of our society" (1). Other scientific bodies have come to similar conclusions. Six major professional societies in the United States— the American Psychological Association, the American Academy of Pediatrics, the American Academy of Child and Adolescent Psychiatry, the American Medical Association, the American Academy of Family Physicians, and

the American Psychiatric Association—recently concluded that "the data point overwhelmingly to a causal connection between media violence and aggressive behavior in some children" (2). In a report on page 2468 of this issue, Johnson and colleagues (3) present important evidence showing that extensive TV viewing among adolescents and young adults is associated with subsequent aggressive acts.

Despite the consensus among experts, lay people do not seem to be getting the message from the popular press that media violence contributes to a more violent society. We recently demonstrated that even as the scientific evidence linking media violence to aggression has accumulated, news reports about the effects of media violence have shifted to weaker statements, implying that there is little evidence for such effects (4). This inaccurate reporting in the popular press may account for continuing controversy long after the debate should have been over, much as the cigarette smoking/cancer controversy persisted long after the scientific community knew that smoking causes cancer.

For these authors, the evidence is overwhelming that media violence is responsible for a more violent society. However, other authors argue that many of the studies of media violence have been flawed or underestimate the pro-social influence of the media.

As Denis McQuail points out (1994:344):

It is sufficient to note the following at this point: the balance of evidence supports the view that media *can* lead to violent behavior and probably have done so; these effects occur mainly as a result of "triggering" of aggressive acts, imitation, identification with aggressive heroes and "desensitization," leading to a higher tolerance for real violence. There are substantial areas of dispute about the extent to which media provide release from aggressive feelings rather than provoke aggressive acts; about the applicability of laboratory findings to natural settings; about the relative importance of fictional versus "real life" portrayal of violence; about whether media can work on their own; and about the overall significance of whatever contribution mass media actually make to the level of violence in society. It should be kept in mind that media can have "pro-social" effects and the basic processes are likely to be the same.

The point is, the argument about media and violence still continues, even though many media researchers would say that violence in the media does contribute to violent behavior in children and others. So who is right—the scholars who have argued that media violence has an impact on people who watch it or those scholars who argue that we must not neglect the cathartic role of the media and that the methodologies used in many violence research projects are flawed?

Ethics and the Media

This discussion of violence in the media is part of a broader topic which deals with ethics and the media. Philosophers have struggled with ethics for thousands of years, defining it and explaining how it works in any number of different areas. Usually there are dilemmas that have to be resolved in an ethical manner, though defining "ethical manner" is extremely difficult. This is because there are many groups which have different ethical standards that are considered valid, and it is difficult to decide what is ethical when you face conflicting arguments.

Violence is only one area of interest to media ethicists. They are also concerned with: the way sexuality is dealt with and, in particular, the exploitation (sexploitation) of women's bodies found in television programs, films, and advertising; the use of stereotypes of different racial, ethnic, and gender groups; and the over-representation of white males and under-representation of women and ethnic and racial groups; the invasion of privacy by some journalists (and now by the National Security Agency); and with bias in news shows. The fact that a small group of individuals own most of the media corporations raises issues of the way the media are used and what stories their news organizations cover and how they cover them. In theory, news organizations should operate in the public interest, but because many of them are part of organizations controlled by a relatively small group of people, some newspapers and news programs can be seen as a kind of manipulation, with a political bias. Thus, the Fox News Network has been attacked as being, in reality, a propaganda arm of the Republican party.

There have been hundreds of studies of violence, and to this date there is little agreement about how to define violence and assess its effects. Whom do we blame for all the violence in the media? What are its effects? How does showing violence in texts relate to freedom of speech? These questions continue to be debated by media ethicists, communications scholars and politicians.

Theories of Mass Communication

The debate about violence and the media suggests that we should think about the media in terms of what they are—forms of mass communication. How we see the media is connected to theories we hold about mass communication. Now that I've offered a timeline on the development of the media and discussed certain problems connected with the effects of the media, I will turn my attention to different theories about the nature of mass communication and its effects that have been offered by scholars. I should point out that there have been many different approaches to the role of media and its relations to mass communication and many theorists of mass communication disagree with one another on the role of media.

We will see that there are many different theories about media and the role they play in our lives and in society. Most media theorists believe that the media are important, but they suggest the media are important in different ways. Marshall McLuhan argues that "the medium is the message," which suggests that the media are more important than the texts they carry. William Stephenson argues that we should see the media as enabling "play" and thus focus our attention on their role in entertaining us and making us feel better about ourselves. For Elizabeth Noelle-Neumann, the media help shape public opinion and generate "**spirals of silence**" on the part of those who feel their views are in the minority. George Gerbner is interested in the way the media—and television in particular—"cultivate" us and provide views of the world that may not be accurate. Television provides skewed pictures of the world with many groups, such as women and people of color, under represented. And Tony Schwartz turns things upside down and suggests that what the media do is strike some kind of a responsive chord with material already in our minds—material that was put there by the media and thus can be accessed by messages that strike responsive chords. Paul Lazarsfeld and Elihu Katz (and others) suggest there is a **two-step flow** that has to be taken into account, and Maxwell McCombs and Donald Shaw write about the way the media shape agendas.

Our first theorist, Marshall McLuhan, is one of the most controversial and enigmatic thinkers. His famous theorem, "the medium is the message," still mystifies many media scholars.

Marshall McLuhan or
The Medium is the Message

Marshall McLuhan (1911–1980) was a Canadian literature scholar who found that he could use mass mediated texts, such as comic strips and advertisements, to interest his students in his theories about media. Many scholars disliked him because of all the attention he got and attacked his work because of his jazzy style of writing, but now he is seen as an extremely important thinker who was ahead of his time—writing about global villages and the power of electronic media.

Marshall
McLuhan

McLuhan argues that the medium is more important than the texts or messages the medium carries because, as he wrote in *Understanding Media* (1965:18), "the effects of technology do not occur at the level of opinions or concepts, but alter sense ratios or patterns of perception steadily and without resistance." That is why he was able to proclaim, enigmatically, that "the medium is the message." Thus, for example, the very nature of print media has certain consequences. Print media, which are linear (we read lines of type) encourages, he suggests, rationality, uniformity, continuity, individualism, and nationalism. He contrasts print with electronic media, which are inclusive and immediate.

Print also fosters standardization, community, nationalism, specialization, the assembly line in factories, and railroads. Electronic media, on the other hand, involve all-at-onceness or simultaneity. Print media and electronic media lead to different sensibilities. Print media tend to focus our minds on classifying data (making sense of what we've read), while electronic media stimulate pattern recognition. I sketch out these differences in this chart—which deals with oppositions I've elicited from his writings.

Print Media	Electronic Media
Eye/Visual	Aural
Linear	All-at-once
Logic	Emotion
Connected	Simultaneous
Rationality	The mythic
The book	The radio
Individualism	Community
Detachment	Involvement
Separation	Connection
Data classification	Pattern recognition

In *Understanding Media,* McLuhan focuses his attention on the media, per se, though in other works, such as *The Mechanical Bride,* he is concerned about what genres of art, like advertisements and comic strips, reveal about American culture and society. Critics who focus on creators and their texts tend to do biographical research. Critics who focus on the impact of texts on audiences or on America (or any society) tend to do sociological research. Many critics focus their attention on texts, the media that carry them, and their impact on audiences and society, at large. Media criticism deals with one or more of these focal points and is not confined to a particular medium, such as television or film or video games.

McLuhan also made a distinction between what he called **"hot" media**, which have a great deal of information, and **"cool" media**, which have little information. As he writes in *Understanding Media* (1965:22–23):

> There is a basic principle that distinguishes a hot medium like radio from a cool one like the telephone, or a hot medium like the movie from a cool one like TV. A hot medium is one that extends one single sense in "high definition." High definition is the state of being filled with data. A photograph is, visually, "high definition." A cartoon is "low definition," simply because very little visual information is provided. Telephone is a cool medium, or one of low definition, because the ear is given a meager amount of information.... Hot media are, therefore, low in participation, and cool media are high in participation or completion by the audience. Naturally, therefore, a hot medium like radio has very different effects on the user from a cool medium like the telephone.

His ideas are shown in this table that I have made, taken from his discussion of the topic in the second chapter of *Understanding Media*.

Hot Media	Cool Media
High definition (full of data)	Low definition (little data)
Low participation (excludes)	High participation (includes)
Movie	Television program
Radio	Telephone
Photograph	Cartoon
Printed word	Speech
Lecture	Seminar
City	Small town

This analysis of hot and cold media explains why we enjoy seminars, where we participate in the class, more than large classes, where we sit and take notes, and why we prefer speech to the printed word.

McLuhan fell into disfavor among many academics for a number of years, but with the development of social media, his ideas about "global villages" now resonate with many scholars and students, and he has become increasingly popular. He talked about the social and cultural significance of things like washing machines, comic strips, and advertisements in his book, *The Mechanical Bride,* published in 1951 and now considered one of the most important analyses of media and popular culture.

McLuhan was a scholar who loved making puns and playing around with language. This playfulness we find in McLuhan is central to our next theorist of mass communication, William Stephenson.

William Stephenson's Play Theory

William Stephenson (1902–1989) developed what he called the "**play theory** of mass communication," which argues that mass communication provides "play" for people and gives them something in common to talk about, which fosters mutual socialization and integration into society. As he writes in his book, *The Play Theory of Mass Communication* (1967:1):

> What, then, can mass communication do? [It is] the thesis of this book that at its best mass communication allows people to become absorbed in *subjective play....* There are some who look with an uneasy eye at these mass pleasures; behind them they see the lurkings of "hidden persuasion" and "tyranny over the mind" (a view expressed by Aldous Huxley). Mankind, these critics feel, is being painlessly put to sleep by the cunning of advertisers and purveyors of mass pap for the public. This, it seems to me, is a jaundiced view.

Many theorists of mass communication have gone wrong, Stephenson asserts, by studying the media as an agent of persuasion rather than an agent of entertainment and pleasure. The critics did this because they didn't recognize the "play" nature of mass communication. One reason media scholars neglected the play aspects of communication was because they tended to focus on the functional aspects of media—that is, its role of stabilizing or destabilizing society

Critics of the Play Theory suggest it focuses too much attention on the subjective aspects of mass communication and its role in leading to self-enhancement and pleasure, both essentially psychological matters, and not enough attention on other dimensions of mass communication, such as its role in politics and society. In contemporary society, when so many young people are wired to their smart phones or MP3 players, the notion that play and entertainment may be of central importance to mass communication doesn't seem unreasonable.

Probably the most widely spread and most often discussed theory of mass communication, "**Cultivation Theory**," was elaborated by George Gerbner, who was the Dean of the Annenberg School for Communication at the University of Pennsylvania and, for many years, editor of *The Journal of Communication*, one of the most influential communication journals. Unlike Stephenson's theory, which presented media exposure in a positive light, Gerbner's theory suggested that media exposure, and especially watching television, had certain negative effects, which I will discuss now.

George Gerbner's Cultivation Theory

George Gerbner (1919–2005) developed what is known as the cultivation theory of the media. His theory focused on television, which he said dominates our symbolic environment and shapes our conception of reality. As he wrote in a classic essay, "Liberal Education in the Information Age" (1983–1984:14–18):

> What is the world according to television like? To discover its main features and functions, we have to look at familiar structures in an unfamiliar light. Rituals rationalize and serve a social order. They make the necessary and inevitable appear natural and right. In conventional entertainment stories, plots perform that rationalizing function. They provide novelty, diversion, and distraction from the constant reiteration of the functions performed by casting, power, and fate. The main points to observe, therefore, are who is who

(number and characterization of different social types in the cast); who risks and gets what (power to allocate resources including personal integrity, freedom of action, and safety); and who comes to what end (fate, or outcomes inherent in the structure that relates social types to a calculus of power, risks and relative success or failure).

People who view a great deal of television tend to believe that the world they see on television is what the real world is like, leading to all kinds of distortions and misconceptions in their thinking about what the world is really like. The television world under represents women, old people, and ethnic minorities and over represents criminals and cops. This leads to people having unreal notions about the amount of crime in society and becoming overly fearful.

Gerbner's theory has been attacked for failing to consider the personalities of the people "cultivated" by television. They may be fearful of the world because of underlying personality problems and not because they've watched a great deal of television. Cultivation theory has also been criticized for assuming that the people who watch television all get the same messages from the texts they see. We know that different people get different things out of the same text, so there are reasons to question the theory's main notion—that watching television gives people unreal views of the world. Gerbner focused on television because it is the dominant medium for most people, who watch television around five hours a day, and cultivation theory is one of the most discussed theories of communication in recent years. We turn now to an important article published in the journal that George Gerbner edited, *The Journal of Communication*. This article deals with the role media play in the creation of public opinion.

Elizabeth Noelle-Neumann's "Spiral of Silence" Theory

A German scholar, Elizabeth Noelle-Neumann (1916–2010), wrote an influential article, "The Spiral of Silence: A Theory of Public Opinion," which suggested that when people think they are in a minority, they tend to keep quiet, while people who think they are in a majority feel confident about making their views known and do so. Members of minorities tend to question the validity of their reasoning and are afraid to speak up lest they isolate themselves from their communities. She discussed what happens when there are conflicts (1974:44):

> He may find himself on one of two sides. He may discover that he agrees with the prevailing (or winning) view, which boosts his self-confidence and enables him to express himself with an untroubled mind and without any danger of isolation, in conversation, by cutting those who hold different views. Or he may find that the views he holds are losing ground; the more this appears to be so, the more uncertain he will become of himself, and the less he will be inclined to express his opinion.

She adds, "Thus the tendency of the one to speak up and the other to be silent starts off a spiraling process which increasingly establishes one opinion as the prevailing one" (44). As a result of this "spiral of silence," we have to hold public opinion suspect, because many people will want to be on what they perceive to be the winning side and will not reveal their beliefs.

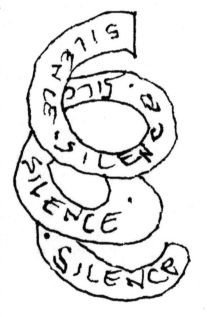

People, then, often overestimate the strength of those who oppose their views and underestimate the strength of those who share their views, and are swayed, due to their fear of becoming isolated. A process is then set in motion in which those with minority views (or views they believe to be minority views) becoming increasingly silent, lest they become isolated and get negative judgments from those holding the majority views. We can describe the "Spiral of Silence" Theory as a social-psychological one, since it suggests that the mass media do not reflect opinion but create it. As Noelle-Neumann writes:

> According to the social-psychological mechanism here called the "spiral of silence," the mass-media have to be seen as creating public opinion; they provide the environmental pressure in which people respond with alacrity, or with acquiescence, or with silence. (1974:51)

Her theory may explain why young people are so concerned about "fitting in" and doing what's popular, or conversely, afraid of being isolated. Noelle-Neumann's theory can be seen as an example of the sociological maxim that people's behavior is based on their perceptions of the world, not on the way the world actually is (to the extent that we can know this, that is).

Noelle-Neumann's theory is about public opinion and the way that it is shaped by the media. People are affected by their estimates of how popular or unpopular some piece of legislation or some political opinion is—based, in large measure, on their exposure to media.

Think, for example, of the power of talk radio, which is mostly conservative in nature. People who only listen to conservative talk radio programs tend to assume their perspective on things is held by most Americans, which is not correct.

She has been accused of over-representing the power of the media. Not everyone gets the same thing from what they see on television and from the other media to which they are exposed. And now, in the internet age, oppositional voices have a good chance of being heard and, occasionally, going viral. When some text goes "viral" on YouTube, it means that its perspective on the world becomes popular and can either provide viewers with a perspective on life that generates some kind of a "spiral of silence" or that attacks those views on the part of those who have different opinions and different tastes. Now that we have social media, people aren't as silent as they once were, and many minority perspectives are available.

The theory I will discuss next, the "Two-Step Flow" theory, argues that our opinions are not shaped directly by our exposure to media, as the "Spiral of Silence" theory suggests, but by "opinion leaders," people whom others respect.

Paul Lazarsfeld and Elihu Katz's "Two-Step Flow" Theory

Paul Lazarsfeld (1901–1976) and Elihu Katz's (1926–) *Personal Influence* (1955) developed a theory which argued that the media don't operate on people directly but on "opinion leaders" who function as intermediaries between the messages in the media and individuals who are members of groups in which they have contact with these opinion leaders. The "Two-Step Flow" theory argues that individuals generally are members of social groups and interact with one another. The response individuals have to mass mediated messages is influenced by others, generally people of higher education and status, who, as "opinion leaders," shape the responses ordinary people have to messages in the media. The first step, then, involves the mass media and opinion leaders, and the second step involves opinion leaders and members of groups to which they belong.

Agenda-Setting theory takes a different approach to the way the media affect people. The focus is not on media's entertainment or play value or the way opinion leaders shape public opinion in a two-step flow. The theory does have similarity to Gerbner's "Cultivation Theory" in that it suggests that what people are exposed to in the media plays an important role in what they think about things. That is, media **gatekeepers**—by focusing on certain topics and neglecting others—set our agendas.

Agenda-Setting Theory

"Agenda-Setting" theory argues that the mass media shape public opinion by paying attention to certain topics and neglecting others. The media, then, set priorities for topics to be concerned about. Two supporters of this theory, Malcolm McCombs and Donald Shaw, explained how it works in an article, "Structuring the 'Unseen Environment'" (1976:18–22):

> Audiences not only learn about public issues and other matters through the media, they also learn how much importance to attach to an issue or topic from the emphasis the mass media place upon it. For example, in reflecting what candidates are saying during a campaign, the mass media apparently determine the important issues. In other words, the mass media set the "agenda" of the campaign. This ability to affect cognitive change among individuals is one of the most important aspects of the power of mass communication.

This theory suggests, then, that the media play an important role in politics by focusing our attention on certain things and thus setting the agenda for topics people think about.

Tony Schwartz's "Responsive Chord" Theory

Finally, I will discuss the ideas of Tony Schwartz (1924–2008), a well known advertising executive and media consultant described by Marshall McLuhan as "the guru of the electronic age." Schwartz developed what is known as the **"responsive chord" theory** of communication. He describes most theories of communication as involving the transportation of messages from one person to another or to many others. His theory is different. He focuses upon the way information found in the media and advertising often strikes a "responsive chord" in people and resonates with them and their beliefs. As he explains (1974:24–25):

> Many of our experiences with electronic media are coded and stored in the same way they are perceived. Since they do not undergo a symbolic transformation, the original experience is more directly available to us when it is recalled. Also, since the experience is not stored in a symbolic form, it cannot be retrieved by symbolic cues. It must be evoked by a stimulus that is coded the same way as the stored information is coded. The critical task is to design our package of stimuli so that it resonates with information already stored within an individual and thereby induces the desired learning or behavioral effect. Resonance takes place when the stimuli put into our communication evoke *meaning* in a listener or viewer.

According to Schwartz, the function of the communicator, in many cases, is not to transfer new information to receivers or audiences, but to strike a responsive chord, utilizing the information they already have stored in their minds. When you make use of some of the information that the people to whom you are communicating already know, you are using media to "press people's buttons," to use popular jargon. This process helps explain how advertising works. The task of the advertiser, according to Schwartz's theory, is not to sell products or services to people by giving them new information, but to do so by striking a responsive chord and using the information people already have.

For example, if a person has been exposed to many messages about Coca-Cola from its advertising, a new advertisement for Coca-Cola strikes a chord with the information stored in that person's unconscious and has a better chance of being persuasive. You are not selling people by providing information as much as reminding them, by striking a responsive chord with information they already possess, to order Coca-Cola next time they want a soft drink.

These views of the media are interesting, controversial, and still relevant, but there has been a big change in our access to sending messages in the media. The growth of social media has led to important changes in the way we use and relate to media, the topic I will discuss in the next chapter.

Applications

1. Which theory of mass communication best explains why people consume so much media? Justify your answer.

2. George Gerbner's cultivation theory is one of the most widely discussed theories. How do contemporary media scholars view his theory? What are its strong points? What criticisms have been made of it?

3. Find two studies of media violence with opposing points of view, and see which one is most convincing.

4. Examine an advertisement or commercial in terms of the "responsive chord" theory. What is in people's minds that responds to messages in the advertisement or commercial?

5. Does conservative right-wing radio foster a "spiral of silence" in liberals? Justify your answer.

Chapter 8

Social Media

Messages: An Introduction to Communication by Arthur Asa Berger, 158–169.

Social Media is a new marketing tool that allows you to get to know your customers and prospects in ways that were previously not possible. This information and knowledge must be paid for with output of respect, trustworthiness, and honesty. Social Media is not a fad, but I also think it's just the beginning of the marketing revolution—not the end.

Marjorie Clayman, Clayman Advertising, Inc.

Social Media are the platforms that enable the interactive web by engaging users to participate in, comment on and create content as means of communicating with their social graph, other users and the public. Social media has the following characteristics:

- Encompasses wide variety of content formats including text, video, photographs, audio, PDF and PowerPoint. Many social media make use of these options by allowing more than one content alternative.

- Allows interactions to cross one or more platforms through social sharing, email and feeds.

- Involves different levels of engagement by participants who can create, comment or lurk on social media networks.

- Facilitates enhanced speed and breadth of information dissemination.

- Provides for one-to-one, one-to-many and many-to-many communications.

- Enables communication to take place in real time or asynchronously over time.

- Is device indifferent. It can take place via a computer (including laptops and netbooks), tablets (including iPads, iTouch and others) and mobile phones (particularly smartphones).

- Extends engagement by creating real-time online events, extending online interactions offline, or augmenting live events online.

Heidi Cohen, heidicohen.com/social-media-definition/

The quotation by Heidi Cohen, a marketing consultant, points out a number of important aspects of social media, many of which involve the way social media can be used to connect people with others and, for marketers, to sell goods and services to people. But, the quotation also deals with many other aspects of social media and its relation to the process of communication.

Statistics on Social Media

This information comes from a PowerPoint presentation by Karen Philips of the T3 agency found on the website of the Advertising Education Foundation on March 4, 2010. The statistics are quite remarkable.

 25% of all internet views are for social networking sites

 800 million Facebook users [now more than a billion]

 133 million blogs indexed since 2002

 9 billion Tweets to date

 50 million Tweets per day

 1 trillion unique URLs in Google's Index

 1 billion video views on YouTube per day

 54% of all internet views are on Facebook

 60 million status updates in more than 65 languages on Facebook every day

Philips suggests that the "Old Media" (television, radio, magazines, newspapers, catalogues, direct mail, billboards) are being eclipsed by the "New Media" (social networking sites, including geo-social networking sites such as Bright Kite, FourSquare, and Gowalta). She notes the following:

70% increased advertising budgets for social media

28% shift from traditional to digital media

41% decrease in print and radio advertising

We can see that the impact of the New Media has hit print advertising very hard, and many newspapers and magazines are now struggling to survive and are looking for new business models to enable them to do so.

The 2014 Pew Internet report on "The Web at 25 in the U.S." offers some other interesting statistics:

87% of American adults use the Internet

50% of American adults have cell phones

58% of American adults have smartphones

85% of American adults use computers

67% of American adults believe the internet strengthens relations with family and friends

Social Media as Connection Rather Than Information

We use the term "social media" to cover recent changes in the communication process made possible by the internet and devices such as smartphones and tablets, and the creation of a number of sites such as Facebook, Twitter, Instagram, Linked-In, YouTube, and Skype, blogs of all kinds, and various other services providing music, films, and videos to people. Earlier I discussed the amount of media eight- to eighteen-year-olds consume—around nine hours per day, to which we must add another hour and a half for texting on their cell phones and smartphones. The Kaiser study did not count cell phone use in its survey, in part because some cell phone use involves listening to music or watching television, but however you calculate things, it is obvious that our eight- to eighteen-year-olds lead media saturated lives.

Bronislaw
Malinowski

We know that a good deal of the ninety minutes teens spend with their cell phones is devoted to texting (and, for a small minority, sexting). Some teens send as many as one hundred texts a day to their friends, which means this activity plays a major role in the social life of these teens. Many of these texts are very brief and contain little information. They can be seen as what the Polish anthropologist Bronislaw Malinowski called "phatic communication" (from the Greek "phatos," or "spoken").

Phatic communication, let us remember, is basically social and not informational speech. The purpose of this communication is to express sociability and strengthen bonds with others. Malinowski described it as follows (quoted in Miller 2011:203):

They fulfill a social function, and that is their principal aim, but they are neither the result of intellectual reflection, nor do they necessarily arouse reflection in the listener. Once again we may say that language does not function here as a means of transmission of thought.

It would seem that maintaining a network of friends is the most important aspect of texting, rather than conveying thought, and so we have teenagers feverishly and mindlessly texting or sending messages by other means, primarily to strengthen their connections with others.

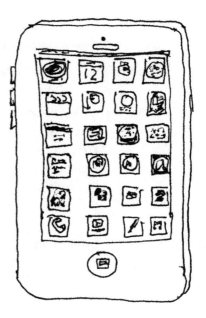

Are Social Media Anti-Social?

There is an element of stress connected with all this texting. Texters are forced, one might say, to keep texting to satisfy the people they are texting, and the people who are texted must keep texting to keep the connections. Sherry Turkle, a professor at the Massachusetts Institute of Technology, was interviewed on the Public Broadcasting Station show, "Fresh Air," about her research on texting. She offers some insights into aspects of the texting phenomenon we don't generally think about and some notions about texting's impact on young people. This summary of her discussion of text messaging explains why she sees texters as "alone together":

> When Turkle asked teens and adults why they preferred text messaging over face-to-face conversation, they responded that when you're face to face, "you can't control what you are going to say, and you don't know how long it's going to take or where it could go." But Turkle believes that these perceived weaknesses of conversation are actually conversation's strengths. Face-to-face interaction teaches "skills of negotiation, of reading each other's emotion, of having to face the complexity of confrontation, dealing with complex emotion," Turkle says. She thinks people who feel they are too busy to have conversations in person are not making the important emotional connections they otherwise would. All this leads to Turkle's theory that it is possible to be in constant digital communication and yet still feel very much alone. In Turkle's interviews with adults and teenagers, she found people of all ages are drawn to their devices for a similar reason: "What is so seductive about texting, about keeping

that phone on, about that little red light on the BlackBerry, is you want to know who wants you," Turkle says.

(www.npr.org/2012/10/18/163098594/in-constant-digi-tal-contact-we-feel-alone-together)

This would suggest that the smartphone may be having a negative impact on the social development of young people, large numbers of whom seem addicted to texting. Texting prevents them from learning how to relate to others directly and having the face-to-face conversations that are so important to their psychological development.

Language Use on Social Media

Texting may be having an impact on the way people communicate, since many text messages use inventive abbreviations of one kind or another, and sometimes just fragments of language. There are an estimated 1,500 abbreviations and the like that people use in texting and sending messages. Below I offer the first text messaging and chat abbreviations that use numbers and characters found on a site listing text message abbreviations.

?	I have a question
?	I don't understand what you mean
?4U	I have a question for you
;S	Gentle warning, like "Hmm? What did you say?"
^^	Meaning "read line" or "message above"
<3	Meaning "sideways heart" (love, friendship)
< 3	Meaning "broken heart"

(Webopdia.com/quick_ref/textmessageabbreviations.ap)

An article in *Harper's* deals with a curious aspect of the way young people text. The author, Joe Pinsker, writes in his article, "Punctuated Equilibrium" (2014):

A battle is being waged over the apostrophe, and the names of two of the online factions—the Apostrophe Protection Society and Kill the Apostrophe—suggest an extremism usually reserved for blood, rather than ink or pixels. The former, founded by a retired British copy editor, provides a gentle guide to deploying the apostrophe. "It is indeed a threatened species!" the site warns, a little preciously. The Web site Kill the Apostrophe, meanwhile, argues that the mark "serves only to annoy those who know how it is supposed to be used and to confuse those who dont [sic]."

But if apostrophes are threatened, it's not just because people don't know how to use them. Smartphone keyboards can make them cumbersome to insert. As Dennis Baron, a professor of English and linguistics at the University of Illinois, notes, adding an apostrophe to a text message usually means toggling from the main keyboard to one that displays punctuation. "It is inconvenient in terms of interrupting the flow of writing," he says.

We can see that young people have developed a number of ways of making texting easier and faster. There is some question about the impact these texting symbols used in chat abbreviations is having on other written forms of communication. When we text, our writing is full of abbreviations. This may be appropriate for texting and messaging, but is it appropriate for term papers and other kinds of academic writing? Texting may also stress texters physically, since it takes a certain amount of effort to send texts, and psychologically, since texters may feel that they must like the right songs, stars, films, and other aspects of pop culture in the texts they send.

The social media create artificial or virtual communities of people, not real communities. I have a number of "friends" and "followers" on Facebook and Twitter, most of whom I've never met. There are, in fact, some people on Facebook and other sites who collect as many "friends" as they can get, for one reason or another. But are these "friends" really friends? I don't think so, though my understanding of friendship is based on having met people in person and on face-to-face communication possibilities and not virtual friendship. Young people, raised on the internet, may have a different notion of what friendship means.

A woman I know has something like 200,000 followers for one of her blogs. She has to work hard to maintain their interest. Her situation suggests that the line between personal blogging and the mass media is now difficult to establish. I have a blog on Facebook called "Arthur Asa Berger and the Literary Life." I use it to write about my activities as a writer, post drawings of culture theorists, offer random speculations on writing, and publicize my books, and there are a few dozen or so people who follow the blog and who sometimes write comments or "like" on something I've posted. I feel a certain amount of pressure generated by my readers—I have to keep coming up with topics they may find interesting, to enter posts of selections from my books they might want to read, and to use images to illustrate my postings. So there are certain obligations and burdens involved in texting and blogging that have to be recognized.

Are Social Media Replacing or Augmenting Mass Media?

It would seem that, for many people, the old mass communication model of a few senders and an enormous number of receivers is no longer correct, since we now have all kinds of different forms of communication facilitated by the internet and the use of smartphones and other devices. But social media have not completely replaced the mass media. Americans still watch an average of around five hours of television each day, but the social media provide alternatives to the mass media that large numbers of people enjoy and considerably facilitate interpersonal and small group communication thanks to email and Skype and other sites and programs.

Facebook provides us with an excellent example of the importance of social media to people in many countries. Facebook now has more than a billion members, and the statistics about its pervasiveness and the amount of time people spend on Facebook are remarkable—and, as one might imagine, of considerable interest to marketers and advertising agencies.

Social media is also of interest to psychologists, psychoanalysts, and many kinds of social scientists who are concerned about the psychological, social, and cultural effects of this new phenomenon. In some cases, theorists have offered ideas about the mind and psyche that we can adapt to understanding new technologies, such as the smartphone, the dominant device in the digital era in which we live.

A Psychoanalytic Perspective on
the Social Media and Smartphones

A smartphone, such as the iconic iPhone or its various Android and now Microsoft competitors, is essentially a powerful minicomputer that we can use to do any number of things—depending on the apps we have. The smartphone is now the most important device many people own; they use it to listen to music, check their e-mail, send text messages, shoot photographs and videos, and call people, among other things. The smartphone is having an impact in many different areas, and smartphones, which often have forty or fifty apps on them, can do any number of things for people, which means owners develop certain dependencies on their smartphones and often have an emotional attachment to them. As a friend of mine put it, "I love my iPhone," and I would imagine many other iPhone and smartphone owners feel the same way. A Nielsen Tech Crunch report gives statistics on smartphone use and the number of apps on a typical smartphone (accessed July 22, 2014):

> With smartphone penetration now at 50 percent in the U.S., the world of apps is seeing a knock-on effect in their popularity: according to a new report from Nielsen, mobile consumers are downloading more apps than ever before, with the average number of apps owned by a smartphone user now at 41—a rise of 28 percent on the 32 apps owned on average last year.
>
> But at the same time, there are hints of people possibly approaching a limit to how much they might use them: despite the rise in app numbers, the amount of time that people are spending on apps has remained essentially flat: collectively, they are being used for 39 minutes per day today, compared to 37 minutes in 2011.
>
> (techcrunch.com/2012/05/16/nielsen-u-s-consumers-app-downloads-up-28-to-41-4-of-the-5-/most-popular-still-belong-to-google)

These figures give us a good idea of the place smartphones have in our lives. Smartphones are of particular importance to teenagers, a topic I will discuss using psychoanalytic theory.

They spend much more than 39 minutes a day with their smartphones—as much as 90 minutes a day texting, playing games, and doing various other things with them.

A prominent psychoanalyst, **Erik Erikson** (1902–1994), wrote a great deal about problems children and adolescents face. His ideas help us understand the attachment of young people to their smartphones. In his book, *Childhood and Society*, he offers an analysis of the problems adolescents face caused by the rapid growth of their bodies and the questions of identity and role confusion they suddenly face. He writes (1963:262):

Erik Erikson

> It is the inability to settle on an occupational identity which disturbs individual young people. To keep themselves together they temporarily over identify, to the point of apparent complete loss of identity, with the heroes of cliques and crowds. This initiates the stage of "falling in love," which is by no means entirely, or even primarily, a sexual matter—except where the mores demand it. To a considerable extent adolescent love is an attempt to arrive at a definition of one's identity by projecting one's diffused ego image on another and by seeing it thus reflected and gradually clarified. This is why so much of young love is conversation.

If conversation is so important to adolescents, as a means of finding and consolidating their identities, we can assume that texting functions the same way conversation does for young people and thus can be seen as, among other things, a means of finding and consolidating a suitable identity. Texting is less direct than face-to-face conversation and allows the texters more control over things. You can send a text at any time without having to worry about whether someone is there to receive it. There's no chance of anyone overhearing you (though, of course, the National Security Agency may be listening in its own curious way). We can consider texting as a kind of virtual conversing, in short segments, most often phatic in nature—but not always. There is also an alienating aspect to texting, for you don't have interactions the way you do when you talk with someone on the telephone or Skype them and may not learn how to communicate well in face-to-face interactions.

Summary

The social media have revolutionized our lives in ways we are only beginning to understand. The invention of the smartphone, which is the way many people access the social media, has had an incredible impact on our everyday lives, since it can be used to send emails, check emails, send photographs, take photographs, make videos, tell us the time, and do many other things. After offering some statistics about social media, I discussed their impact on our media (are the social media replacing traditional media?), culture, and society. I discussed texting and how it has impacted on personal relationships. I also offered a psychoanalytic interpretation, using the theories of Erik Erikson, of the role the social media and smartphones play in the lives of people.

Applications

1. Do you think the language used in texting is having negative or positive effects on the way people communicate with one another? Justify your position.

2. Spend a day tracking your use of smartphones and social media. How many text messages did you send? Receive? How much time did you spend with social media sites such as Facebook or Twitter? How many times did you check your email and messages? What does this say about you as a user of social media?

3. Is Sherry Turkle correct when she suggests we are "alone together?" Explain your answer.

4. What is the relationship between social media and the mass media. How has social media affected your consumption patterns of mass media? What does the research show as to how common or uncommon your new pattern is?

Chapter 9

Nonverbal and Visual Communication

Messages: An Introduction to Communication by Arthur Asa Berger, 170–197.

Although "language" often comes to mind when considering communication, no discussion of communication is complete without the inclusion of nonverbal communication. Nonverbal communication has been referred to as "body language" in popular culture since the publication of Julius Fast's book of the same name in 1970. Researchers, however, have defined nonverbal communication as encompassing almost all of human communication except the spoken and written word.... We also define nonverbal communication as *the transfer and exchange of messages in any and all modalities that do not include words.* As we discuss shortly, one of the major ways by which nonverbal communication occurs is through *nonverbal behaviors,* which are behaviors that occur during communication that do *not* include verbal language. But our definition of nonverbal communication implies that it is more than body language. It can be the distance people stand apart when they converse. It can be the sweat stains in their armpits. It can be the design of the room. Nonverbal communication is a broader category than nonverbal behavior, encompassing the way you dress, the place of your office within a larger building, the use of time, the bumper stickers you place on your car, or the arrangement, lighting, or color of your room.

> David Matsumoto, Mark G. Frame, Hyi Sung Hwang,
> eds., *Nonverbal Communication: Science and Applications*

In this chapter I will deal with two aspects of communication: first I will consider the way individuals communicate with others nonverbally, and then I will discuss images and their role in the communication process. I will consider images in dreams and the functions of images in advertising, religion, politics, and personal identity.

It is possible to expand the term "message" to deal with nonverbal communication or "signs," such as facial expressions, body language, hair styles, clothes, props (eyeglasses, handbags, rings), and status symbols (such as mansions or "trophy wives"). Much nonverbal communication is unconscious. How people "read" these messages, including the ones we don't realize we are sending, is a subject of considerable importance and is one of the subtexts of this book. Not only are we always sending messages to others, others are always sending messages to us, even if nobody says a word. In certain circumstances, not saying anything can also be a message—such as when someone says "Do you love me?" to someone else and there's no reply. Chapter 5 on interpersonal communication raised some of the issues that I will deal with again in this chapter.

A considerable amount of the information we get about people comes from nonverbal communication—which we can define as the exchange of information through facial expression, body language, and other physical signs that we learn to interpret as we grow up in society. As I explained in Chapter 3, signs are anything that can be used to stand for something else. For example, when people frown, we usually interpret that frown as a sign that suggests they are not happy about something, and when people smile, we interpret that smile as a sign that they are happy about something. But that is not always the case. A smile can mean many things. The problem is that signs can be ambiguous and can be used to mislead us. That is, as Umberto Eco explained to us earlier in the book, we can lie with signs.

Let's take a look now at some nonverbal signs that send messages to others about who we are and what we are like. I begin with hair styles.

Hair Styles

Each hair style suggests something different to us. We interpret long hair differently from short hair in women and men, and think that men with comb overs are frauds. Punk hair styles and Mohawk hair styles convey certain attitudes about society. Facial hair, such as beards and mustaches, also convey meanings about masculinity and virility, among other things.

In an article in the *San Francisco Chronicle*, "Office Life: Executives Can Lose by a Hair" (1980), Donald White, the business editor, dealt with hair styles and the business world. The article was based on a poll of 200 hair stylists in the San Francisco Bay area about the worst hair styles of business executives. The article appeared many years ago but the insights it offers are still valid. Based on the findings of this poll, I made the following chart, which reflects commonly held opinions and attitudes about the messages conveyed by different hair styles:

Male Hair Styles	Meaning of Hair Styles
Hair parted to hide baldness	Phoniness, self-consciousness
Shoulder length hair	Anti-establishment values
Greased hair	Too slick, not trustworthy
Curly permanent grown out	Sloppy, disinterested
Crew cut	Old fashioned, inflexible

Female Hair Styles	Meaning of Hair Styles
Punk Rock	Anti-authority, belligerence
Back-combed, bouffant	Archaic, can't embrace new ideas
Feathered in front, long in back	Teeny-Bopper, lack of maturity
Severely streaked	Cheapness, low morals
Long hair, same length all around	Lack of personality and warmth

Our hair styles, we see, are messages about our status and personalities that we send to others. Whether they interpret them correctly is another matter.

Facial Expression

These photos by Irfan Essa of different facial expressions also show, in the images below each expression, the energy expended to generate the expression. There are eight universal facial expressions according to Paul Ekman, a psychologist who taught at the University of California and has studied facial expression for many years. The eight universal facial expressions are:

1. anger
2. determination
3. disgust
4. fear
5. neutral
6. pouting
7. sadness
8. surprise

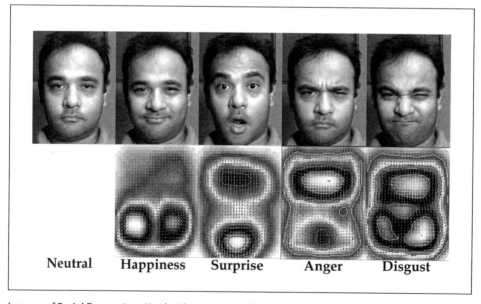

Images of Facial Expression. *Used with permission of Irfan Essa. Copyright © Irfan Essa*

There are many other facial expressions, but they are not universal. Poker players are always scanning the faces of the people they are playing with for "tells," facial expressions, changes in facial color, or changes in the size of pupils (enlarged or dilated) in eyes for information about how good a player's hand is. And we are always looking at the facial expressions of people we are with to see what their expressions may reveal, but we can't be sure that our interpretation of a person's facial expression is correct.

Gestures

Gestures we make with our hands and fingers and limbs, and in some cases by other means, are an important element of communication in many countries. There are one-hand gestures, two-hand gestures, and in some cases, like shrugging our shoulders, part of the body gestures. There are two kinds of gestures—those that we make when we are talking, known as "illustrators," and those we make independent of talking, called "emblems." An Italian scholar, Isabella Poggi, has identified approximately 250 gestures that Italians use in their everyday conversations. The chart that follows, which I compiled from an article about her work, describes a number of the gestures Italians make and tells their meaning.

Gesture	Meaning
Fingers pinched against the thumb	I wasn't born yesterday
Hand circling slowly	Whatever or That will be the day
Index finger twisted against cheek	Something tastes good
Tapping one's wrist	Hurry Up
Hands placed in prayer	What do you expect me to do about it?
Fingers brushing the chin	I don't give a damn

There are also some widely used emblems, such as thumbs up, which means "very good," and making a "V" with one's fingers that means "victory." Emblems are specific to cultures. For example, in America we point with our index fingers, while in Japan people point with their middle finger. As a result of the spread of mass media, some emblems are becoming recognized and adopted in many countries.

What we learn from this discussion of gesture is that conversations can be both verbal and nonverbal at the same time—the gestures reinforcing and perhaps intensifying (or undercutting) the language used. It is common for people to gesture when they speak, but the amount of gesturing varies considerably by country.

Body Language

The way people communicate with their bodies conveys messages to us. Thus, if you are having a conversation with someone, and he or she gives you "the shoulder" (turns away from you), you get the sense they would rather be talking with someone else. Our bodies provide information to others about our sex, age, race, self-confidence, status, and many other things. We also convey information about ourselves by our posture. As David Matsumoto and Hyi Sung Hwang explain in "Body and Gestures," a chapter in a book titled *Nonverbal Communication: Science and Applications* (2013:87):

> Postures communicate attitudinal states and general affect, as opposed to the very specific emotions communicated by face and voice. These attitudinal and general affective states include preference (liking versus disliking), orientation (closed or open), and attention (direct or indirect). These various dimensions can be summarized as communicating general positivity as well as status relationships.... For example, body orientation—the degree to which a person's shoulders and legs are turned in the direction rather than away from another interactant—is associated with attitude toward the interactant; the least direct orientation occurs for disliked interactants while more direct orientations occurs for liked others.

Even our teeth convey information about us. In an article in the *Wall Street Journal* that appeared a number of years ago, a cosmetic dentist argued that people judge us by our teeth, and that professional people who wished to succeed had better make certain that their teeth were white and straight. When we smile, the dentist suggested, people unconsciously react to our teeth, and if they aren't white and straight, they see us in a negative light.

Fashion

The kind of clothes we wear and the styles and brands of our clothes send messages to others about what kind of person we are and what our status is—or, more precisely, what our claim to status is. Fashion is a social institution that exerts a coercive force on us. People scan our shirts and ties and dresses and shoes for cues about our taste and socio-economic status. Some people dress down—below their status—while others dress up, above their status. So we have to be careful when we analyze clothes to make sure we are not being led astray by poseurs. There are an enormous number of "looks" we can adopt in our quest for an identity: preppy, beatnik, dandy, beachnik, biker, hippy, barbarian, ad infinitum. In his 1969 book, *Collective Search for Identity,* sociologist Orrin Klapp discusses a southern California gang called the Broadway Riders, who wear black leather jackets, boots, have long and unkempt hair, earrings, and otherwise look like bikers, but who, for one reason or another, don't have motorcycles. They are, as he puts it, "motorcyclists *without motorcycles."*

I use the term "props" for objects we may wear or carry, such as earrings, eyeglasses, wristwatches, sunglasses, handbags, messenger bags, and so on—each of which is meant to convey some kind of an impression to others based on the brands of the objects and their styling. Now, in the smartphone era, we can add smartphones to the list of props. Props not only convey information to others but also serve to help us consolidate our identities, since branding plays an important role in our selection of props.

What I have dealt with to this point focuses on various aspects of nonverbal communication as it relates to interactions between people. Thus, I've written about topics such as body language, facial expression, and gestures. Now I will move to a more general analysis of visual communication, at a higher level of abstraction, with a discussion of two different ways of perceiving the world—"**haptics**" and "**optics**."

Haptics and Optics

"Haptics," we can say, involves touch and texture, while "optics" involves surfaces and outlines. There is an excellent discussion of the difference between optics and haptics in Claude Gandelman's enigmatically titled book, *Reading Pictures, Viewing Texts.* He discusses the difference between the two (1991:5):

> The two fundamental categories, according to art historian Alois Riegl, one of the great precursors of the semiotic approach to the visual arts, are optics and haptics. Riegl stated that one type of artistic procedure, which corresponds to a certain way of looking, is based on the scanning of objects

according to their outlines. This trajectory of the regard Riegl called the optical. The opposite type of vision, which focuses on surfaces and emphasizes the value of the superficies of objects, Riegl called the haptical (from the Greek *haptein,* "to seize, grasp," or *haptikos,* "capable of touching").... The optical eye merely brushes the surfaces of things. The haptic or tactile eye penetrates in depth, finding its pleasure in texture and grain.

We can see these relationships more clearly in the chart that I have created, based on material in Gandelman's book.

Optic	Haptic
Surface	Depth
Scans outlines	Examines texture and grain
Linearity	Pictorial
Looks	Touches

Vision, Gandelman suggests, can be seen as a form of touching. When we look at an image, we scan it in the form of very quick eye movements, called saccades, which focus on the outline of the image. This same process takes place when we read a poem or some other literary text—our eyes jump around: our optic vision moves around from one part of the image or text to another, and our haptic vision examines the text more carefully.

When we touch one another, we are communicating haptically, and touch, as we all have experienced, can be gentle and soothing, loving (a caress or a hug), or harsh and intimidating (grabbing someone's arm or punching someone). There is ritual touching, as when we shake hands with people when we meet them or say goodbye to them. Touch, then, becomes an important element in the repertoire of communication methods. Kissing is a sexual form of haptic communication, and tickling is generally a "fun" form of haptic communication.

Proxemics

The term "proxemics" was invented by an anthropologist, Edward T. Hall, who defined the term on the first page of his book, *The Hidden Dimension*. He writes in his chapter titled "Culture as Communication" (1969:1):

> The central theme of this book is social and personal space and man's perception of it. Proxemics is the term I have coined for the interrelated observations and theories of man's use of space as a specialized elaboration of culture.
>
> The concepts developed here did not originate with me. Over fifty-three years ago, Franz Boas laid the foundation of the view which I hold that communication constitutes the core of culture and indeed of life itself.

He then discusses the Sapir-Whorf hypothesis (see Chapter 2) that argues that language is more than a medium for expressing thought but is, actually, *"a major element in the formation of thought."* The thesis of his book, Hall explains, is that the "principles laid down by Whorf and his fellow linguists in relation to language apply to the rest of human behavior as well—in fact, to all culture" (1969:2).

This leads Hall to discuss a variety of topics relating to spatiality, such as animal territoriality, visual and auditory space, the language of space, and the way different cultures use space, including what they each regard as a normal distance between two people having a conversation. He discusses intimate distance, personal distance, and social distance, and offers fascinating studies of the way people in different cultures use space. He points out that the Japanese name intersections in cities, rather than the streets leading into them, that there is no Japanese word for privacy, and that the interval, the "ma," is basic to Japanese spatial experience. Arabs use space quite differently and prefer large spaces and high ceilings in their rooms, but avoid partitions because Arabs do not like to be alone.

Hall concludes by suggesting that everything we do is connected to the way we experience space and the various components of space: visual, auditory, olfactory, and thermal. As anyone who has been in a gigantic cathedral recognizes, spatiality has an effect on our emotions and thought processes, and anyone who has traveled to different cultures will recognize that people in one country use space differently than people in another country. When two people have a conversation, the distance they set between them, at which they feel comfortable, is connected to codes they have learned in their cultures.

Now that I've discussed important nonverbal aspects of communication, such as hair style, facial expression, gestures, body language, and proxemics, I will move on to another important element of nonverbal communication—images, and in particular, images with models found in advertisements and television commercials. We can apply what we have learned about hair styles and other matters to the images of the models we find in advertising texts.

Seeing

Seeing is actually a complex process, but it is quite natural because of the remarkable qualities of our eyes. The human eye has a retina, which is the part of the eye sensitive to light; it, in turn, is composed of three parts: the fovea, the macula, and a section of the eye devoted to peripheral vision. Each of these parts is specialized, and together they permit us to see things somewhat differently, but they blend into one another when we look at something.

Nicholas Mirzoeff describes the physical nature of the eye in the introduction to his book, *An Introduction to Visual Culture* (1999:5): "According to one recent estimate, the retina contains 100 million nerve cells capable of about 10 billion processing

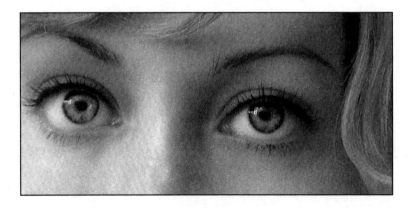

operations per second." This means that our eyes function like supercomputers. Donis A. Dondis (1924–1984), a designer and for many years a professor at Boston University, explains that we do many different things when we see something. She writes in her book, *A Primer of Visual Literacy* (1973:17):

> When we see, we are doing many things at once. We are seeing an enormous field peripherally. We are seeing in an up-to-down, left-to-right movement. We are imposing on what we are isolating in our field of vision not only implied axes to adjust balance, but also a structural map to chart and measure the action of the compositional forces that are so vital to content and, therefore, to message input and output. All of this is happening while at the same time we are decoding all manner of symbols.

Perception, then, involves a number of different operations and involves actions, by us, in focusing on certain things available to us and not paying attention to other things.

Our sense of sight operates "selectively" according to Rudolph Arnheim, a visual communications theorist. E. H. Gombrich, another writer, makes the same point in his classic book, *Art and Illusion*. He explains (1960:172):

> Visual perception is not a passive recording of stimulus material but an active concern of the mind. The sense of sign operates selectively. The perception of shape consists in the application of form categories, which can be called visual concepts because of their simplicity and generality. Perception involves problem solving.

We learn from these writers that perception is not automatic; we focus on some things and neglect other things when we look at anything. In a sense, we can say that you have to look for something in order to see it.

Scientists now estimate that 75 percent of the information that we get is from our eyes and that approximately 40 percent of the fibers that enter or leave our central nervous systems are in our optic nerves. Although we have 100 million sensors in the retina, we only have 5 million channels to our brains from our retinas, so a great deal of information processing is done in our eyes and not in our brains. As I explained earlier, when we look at an object, our eyes make numerous quick movements—called saccades—of about one twentieth of a second. This is the same amount of time devoted to vision persistence, the process that we use to connect frames of a film and see them as continuous.

Psychologist Robert Ornstein explains the way we create our awareness from the different inputs we get (1972:37):

> If we "saw" an image on our retina, the visual world would be different each second, sometimes one object, then another, sometimes a blur due to our eyes moving, sometimes darkness due to blinks. We must then construct a personal consciousness from the selected input, and in this way achieve some stability of awareness out of the rich and constantly changing flow of information reaching our receptors.

This means that, in a sense, we have to construct the world we see. Seeing may be automatic, but we have to focus our attention on certain aspects of things we see and neglect others.

Images

Images can be defined as representations of reality. *The Random House Dictionary of the English Language: The Unabridged Edition* offers twenty different definitions of the term "image." The first definition is: "1. a physical likeness or representation of a person, animal, or thing, photographed, painted, sculptured or otherwise made visible." Another definition points out that images can also be mental representations of things. The twentieth definition is "to resemble." We also see the word image in "imagine" and "imagination," which suggests that we may think in terms of images. The term "image" comes from the

Latin term *imago,* which means a copy or likeness. The image that precedes this section shows, among other things, how fashion differs in two cultures.

When we look at a photograph, we are seeing an image of something or someone, and when we watch television or films, we are seeing visual images formed by photographs, in the case of films, and collections of pixels in the case of television. Remember that in Chapter 7 we noted that adults watch screens of one kind or another for more than eight hours each day, which means we spend a great deal of time looking at images.

Paul Messaris makes an important point in his book, *Visual Persuasion: The Role of Images in Advertising.* He writes (1997:vi):

> Photographs and images on video are typically seen as direct copies of reality. This quality strengthens the viewer's illusion of interacting with real-world people and places, and it also does something else. In many ads, the use of photographs and video serves as evidence that what is being shown in the ad really did happen.... Of course, that kind of evidence may be quite illusory, especially in an age in which photographs can be manipulated so easily by computer.

This kind of manipulation means that photographs no longer serve as evidence, since they can be changed in many different ways, and many films are full of computer-simulated events. Images in the digital age, as we have learned, can lie. We also have long recognized that what a photographer selects and excludes in an image plays a role in the way we think about things.

Understanding the Meaning of an Image

Now that we understand the complexities of the process of seeing and the role of images in our lives, it is interesting to consider how to analyze images, remembering what semiotic theory taught us—that signs have signifiers (sounds and images) and signifieds (concepts linked to the signifiers).

From a semiotic perspective, an image is a collection of signs, and some of those signs are symbols whose meaning has to be learned. We might say that everything in an image is a sign or a sign inside a bigger sign. Thus, for example, suppose we have an advertisement for champagne in a magazine that shows a glass of champagne. It will also show that the champagne in the glass is a light yellow color and there are little bubbles in the champagne. These bubbles and the yellow color function as what I call *signemes,* which are the most fundamental or basic signs within larger signs.

Let us take an advertisement with some people in it and written material as a text to be analyzed. Here are some of the topics, many dealt with earlier in our discussion of nonverbal communication, that might be addressed. You can apply them to the Piccolino ad shown earlier.

1. The product being advertised and its social and cultural significance.

2. The arguments made in the written material for the object.

3. Rhetorical aspects of the written material. Metaphors? Similes?

4. Polar Oppositions found in images used and/or ad copy.

5. The spatiality of the ad. Is it empty or full of material?

6. The kind of balance: axial or dynamic.

7. The focus used in the ad.

8. The use of color in the ad. What colors are used and why?

9. The typefaces used in the written material in the ad.

10. The body types of the models in the ad.

11. The hair colors of the models.

12. The body language of the models.

13. Their facial expressions.

14. The clothes the models are wearing.

15. Props the models have, like sunglasses, hats, jewelry, and so on.

16. Symbols used in the ad. What are they and what function do they have?

17. The target audience of the ad.

You can see from this list that analyzing an advertisement—or any other visual texts such as paintings and photographs—can be a complicated matter and one which involves many different things to think about. From a semiotic perspective, we can ask: Are there any icons in the text? Are there any indexical relationships to consider? Are there any symbols in the text? If so, of what, and what significance do the symbols have? Are there cultural codes that we bring to analyzing a given text?

As Stuart Hall, one of the founders of cultural criticism, explains in his book, *Representations: Cultural Representations and Signifying Practices* (1997:36):

> The underlying argument behind the semiotic approach is that, since all cultural objects convey meaning, and all cultural practices depend on meaning, they must all make use of signs, and in so far as they do, they must work like language works, and be amenable to analysis which basically makes use of Saussure's linguistic concepts...his idea of underlying codes and structures, and the arbitrary nature of the sign.

Of course, there is a difference between knowing how to analyze advertisements and commercials and being able to do so. We have to recognize, also, that some images are very powerful—such as the 2001 images of the World Trade Center towers falling after being hit by planes guided by suicide pilots. Those images were so strong that many psychiatrists advised parents not to let their young children be exposed to them.

Sigmund Freud on Images in Dreams

Sigmund Freud suggested that our dreams are composed of images that we merge together in our dream work and use when recounting a dream. So in our sleep, when we dream, we encounter images. Dreams are like slide shows—we see discrete images, but we put them together to form a narrative. Dreams are generally full of sexual symbols that connect to unconscious or repressed elements in our psyches. We disguise the sexual content of our dreams so our dream sensor won't wake us up. For Freud, dreams are the royal road to the unconscious. As he explained in his masterwork, *The Interpretation of Dreams* (1901/1965:82–83):

Dreams think essentially in images; and with the approach of sleep it is possible to observe how, in proportion as voluntary activities become more difficult, involuntary ideas arise, all of which fall into the class of images.... The transformation of ideas into hallucinations is not the only respect in which dreams differ from corresponding thoughts in waking life. Dreams construct a *situation* out of these images.

The dreams we have, then, are connected to desires and impulses we have, generally of a sexual nature, which we disguise in varying ways. What is remarkable is that these dreams seem real to us while we are having them, because while asleep, we have nothing to compare them with. This may help explain why films seem so real to us—they are like dreams and we become captives who become immersed in the films the way we do when dreaming.

Elements of Images

The basic element of images is the dot—now called, in the digital age, the pixel. Dots can be combined into lines, which are elements in which the dots are not distinguishable or are also seen as the edge of shapes. Lines form shapes. The most basic shapes are triangles, squares, and circles—each of which has certain properties. All other shapes are made of combinations of the three basic shapes. Our visual system "imagines" lines between

PANTS MADE TO A DIFFERENT VISION.

Optical
Illusion

dots that form basic shapes and also plays tricks on us when we
see optical illusions such as the one found in this Levi's ad.

Shapes are made by creating lines or from other phenomena,
as we see in the figure-ground image which can be seen as either
a vase or two profiles, but not both together. Shapes have, in
themselves, certain psychological qualities. They are described
by Dondis as follows (1973:44):

> Each of the basic shapes has its own unique character and
> characteristics and to each is attached a great deal of mean-
> ing, some through association, some through arbitrary
> attached meaning, and some through our own psychological
> and physiological perceptions. The square has associated to its
> dullness, honesty, straightness, and workmanlike meaning;
> the triangle, action, conflict, tension; the circle, endlessness,
> warmth, protection.

If Dondis is correct, shapes by themselves can generate emotions in people who view them.

Lines can be combined in various ways to create certain shapes that have volume—that move from being two dimensional images to three dimensional ones. In our everyday lives, we are familiar with objects that have volume and so impose upon two-dimensional drawings using lines, in certain cases, a third dimension. When dealing with images, spatiality is very important. For example, advertisements for upscale and expensive products generally are simple or empty, not full of objects or people. The code for upscale product advertisements is simplicity and empty space. We can contrast that code with the one for supermarket ads and inexpensive products: no empty space. As we grow up, we are exposed to the different spatial codes in advertising and learn to associate empty space with upscale and expensive products.

We use the term "composition" to deal with the arrangement of elements in an advertisement or photograph or any kind of imaged text. In addition to spatiality, we can consider:

Balance: axial or asymmetrical

Direction: the way elements in an image lead our eyes in certain directions

Lighting: flat or with strong lights and darks, called chiaroscuro

Proportion: the size of different elements in relation to one another

Color: the ways colors are used to create certain feelings and emotions

We can see that images, in themselves, are very complicated. When you combine images, as in television program and films, you enhance the power of the images. The Russian film-maker and film theorist Sergei Eisenstein developed the notion of the "montage," which he explained in his book, *Film Form* (1949:49), as "an idea that arises from the collision of independent shots—shots even opposite to one another." For all practical purposes, we can say that one shot or frame in a film is a photograph, but when you combine shots in certain kinds of sequences, you generate ideas and emotional responses in people exposed to them.

The Functions of Images

Let me suggest, here, some of the different ways in which images can be used. They play an important role in advertising, in religions, in politics, and in our forming our "looks." I begin with advertising, a topic I addressed earlier in my discussion of analyzing an image.

Advertising

Paul Messaris suggests there are three important roles of images in advertising. As he explains in his book on visual persuasion (1997: vii):

> I have outlined three major roles that visual images can play in an ad. They can elicit emotions by simulating the appearance of a real person or object; they can serve as photographic proof that something really did happen; and they can establish an implicit link between the thing that is being sold and some other image(s).

As I explained earlier, film theorists talk about montage, which refers to the way a sequence of images in films can generate emotions in viewers of the film. This helps explain why television commercials can be so powerful. It is no accident that many film directors got their start directing television commercials and why some great film directors, such as Ridley Scott, created remarkable television commercials, such as his classic "1984" commercial for the Macintosh computer.

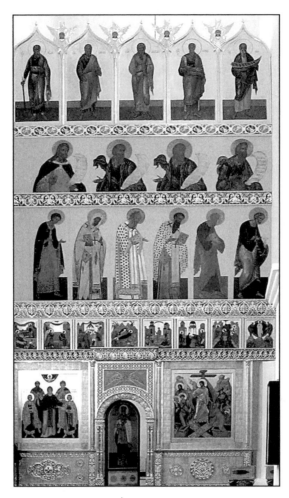

Photo of icons by
Arthur Asa Berger

Religion

All religions appreciate the power of images and use them in
their ceremonies and celebrations and in their churches, syn-
agogues, temples, and mosques (which use only certain kinds
of images since they cannot show the human body). Christian
churches often have paintings of Jesus and various saints. Russian
Orthodox churches are full of ikons of Christ and saints; they
cover almost all of the walls. We see impression management,
related to image-building, in the clothes religious leaders wear,
in the objects they use, and in the design of religious buildings,
like cathedrals, which are designed to produce powerful emotional responses in people attending services.

Politics

Politicians recognize the power of imagery, which explains why they make certain that they have flags and use other patriotic symbols when possible. The camera angles at which a politician is shown generate different effects. Shots in which the camera is below politicians (call "low angle"), so we look up to them, make them appear more powerful. This calls to mind the way, when we were small children, we looked up to our parents, who were much taller than we were. Conversely, shots taken above politicians make them seem weaker, since we are looking down on them. These different shots affect our feelings of safety and vulnerability. If we feel vulnerable, we like to have someone powerful to look after us.

President Obama

The "look" of a politician also is important. Politicians have to figure out a way to look powerful yet not seem distant or aloof. They must appear strong but also appeal to the common man and woman. We see the power of images in politics very clearly in the presidential conventions held every four years. In these conventions, flags and other patriotic symbols are used extensively and the kind of stage and kind of shots used on television all play an important role in our political system.

Personal Identity

I dealt with identity in the first part of this chapter, but here I would like to offer more thoughts on how people decide upon a "look." I would suggest that we decide upon a look after seeing various actors and actresses in television shows and films, being exposed to advertisements in newspapers and magazines, seeing celebrities and famous people on news programs and other kinds of programs, and determining that we'd like to wear certain clothes, have our hair styled in certain ways, and do many other things based on some combination we put together—always, of course, subject to change.

As we get older, we often switch looks. We may be "Goth" in our early teens and become "Preppy" when we go to college.

Different colleges have different looks, also. And at some schools, anything goes. When I taught at San Francisco State University, we had preppies, punks, Goths, bikers, surfers, and students with all kinds of other looks. Postmodern theorists have argued that in postmodern societies, such as we have in the United States, our "looks" and identities are constantly changing. Identity, as reflected in our clothes, our hair styles, our sunglasses, and everything else, is always subject to revision.

I had a student who was obsessed with Polo products and based his whole identity on buying and wearing Polo brand clothes. He wrote about his passion for Polo in a journal he kept on popular culture that was a course assignment. Brands play an important role in the images many people create for themselves because they communicate certain things about people who wear a particular brand of clothes and now, as brands extend themselves, watches, fragrances, sunglasses, eyeglasses, and so on. We choose brands on the basis of the stories these brands create for us in their advertisements and the kinds of models shown in these advertisements.

Visual Culture

This discussion of visual communication has demonstrated the important role images of all kinds play in our lives. Visual communication has become so important that a number of media scholars now use the term "visual culture" to describe contemporary culture. Thus, Nicholas Mirzoeff writes (1999:1):

> Modern life takes place onscreen. Life in industrialized countries is increasingly under constant video surveillance from cameras in buses and shopping malls, on highways and bridges, and next to ATM cash machines. More and more people look back, using devices ranging from traditional cameras to camcorders and Webcams. At the same time, work and leisure are increasingly centered on visual media, from computers to Digital Video Disks.

Mirzoeff quotes a figure of 23 million Americans being online in 1998. Had he written his book in 2013, he could note that more than a billion people are on Facebook and millions of people send four-hundred million Tweets on Twitter every day.

Contemporary societies are visual societies in which a great deal of people's work and leisure is dominated by visual media which are on the screens we gaze at hour after hour. The big change that has taken place in recent years is that the mass media—with a few senders and millions of receivers—no longer have a monopoly on mass communications the way they did, and millions of people now communicate with others in any number of different ways: on blogs, in text messages, by sending Tweets (and images on those Tweets, thanks to applications such as Tweetpic), by taking digital photographs (or videos) and sending them directly from their smartphones or cameras to Facebook.

This book on communication started with the word but it ends with the image, which plays a major role in our visual cultures and now, to a considerable degree, dominates our lives. "In the beginning was the Word" (John 1:1), but now, in the present time, we are all under the spell of the image.

Applications

1. Gustav Le Bon, an important French sociologist, wrote about the role images play in the way crowds function. Here is what he wrote 1895/1960:68:

   > Crowds being only capable of thinking in images are only to be impressed by images. It is only images that terrify or attract them and become motives of action. For this reason theatrical representations, in which the image is shown in its most clearly visible shape, always have an enormous influence on crowds. Bread and spectacular shows constituted for the plebeians of ancient Rome the ideal of happiness, and they asked for nothing more. Nothing has a greater effect on the imagination of crowds in every category than theatrical representations.

   What evidence is there to support Le Bon's ideas? What evidence is there to suggest he was incorrect about crowds only being affected by images? Is there a difference between a crowd and an audience? Explain your answer.

2. Make a photo exhibition of the use of images in houses of worship for various religions. Did you find anything in common in them? If so, how do you explain this? If not, why is this the case?

3. Make a list of all the "looks" you've had in recent years. Describe each of your looks and explain why you chose each look and how the look affected your image of yourself and your relationships with others.

4. Deconstruct the ad shown on the next page or an ad supplied by your instructor. List the signifiers and signifieds in the image and in the textual material.

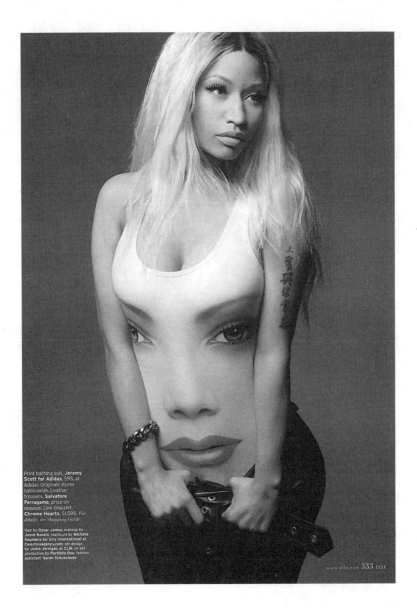

Print bathing suit, **Jeremy Scott for Adidas**, $95, at Adidas Originals stores nationwide. Leather trousers, **Salvatore Ferragamo**, price on request. Link bracelet, **Chrome Hearts**, $1,595. *For details, see Shopping Guide.*

Hair by Oscar James; makeup by Joyce Bonelli; manicure by Michelle Saunders for Orly International at Celestineagency.com; set design by Juliet Jernigan at CLM; on-set production by Portfolio One; fashion assistant: Sarah Schussheim

www.elle.com 333 ELLE

Chapter 10

PUBLIC SPEAKING

Messages: An Introduction to Communication by Arthur Asa Berger, 198–215.

1. Know your material. Pick a topic you are interested in. Know more about it than you include in your speech. Use humor, personal stories and conversational language—that way you won't easily forget what to say.

2. Practice. Practice. Practice! Rehearse out loud with all equipment you plan on using. Revise as necessary. Work to control filler words. Practice, pause and breathe. Practice with a timer and allow time for the unexpected.

3. Know the audience. Greet some of the audience members as they arrive. It's easier to speak to a group of friends than to strangers.

4. Know the room. Arrive early, walk around the speaking area and practice using the microphone and any visual aids.

5. Relax. Begin by addressing the audience. It buys you time and calms your nerves. Pause, smile and count to three before saying anything. ("One one-thousand, two one-thousand, three one-thousand. Pause. Begin.) Transform nervous energy into enthusiasm.

6. Visualize yourself giving your speech. Imagine yourself speaking, your voice loud, clear and confident. Visualize the audience clapping —it will boost your confidence.

7. Realize that people want you to succeed. Audiences want you to be interesting, stimulating, informative and entertaining. They're rooting for you.

8. Don't apologize for any nervousness or problem—the audience probably never noticed it.

9. Concentrate on the message—not the medium. Focus your attention away from your own anxieties and concentrate on your message and your audience.

(www.toastmasters.org/tips.asp)

Toastmasters International, an organization devoted to helping people become good public speakers—whose advice on public speaking is cited above—was founded to solve the problem that speaking in public is said to be one of the most anxiety-producing activities for most people. That is because they fear they will bore others, that they have nothing interesting to say, and that people to whom they are speaking may show signs of displeasure, heckle them, or even get up and walk out of the room where they are speaking. These acts humiliate us and attack our sense of self, but this kind of behavior is very rare. After learning a few essential tricks of the trade and practicing a bit, most people can do a decent job of public speaking. One secret is to be yourself and draw upon your own sense of humor and your style of doing things.

Public Speaking as a Performance

It is useful to think of public speaking as a kind of performance and you as an actor or actress who has to keep the attention of your audience for an hour—or whatever period of time you have with them. Audiences are fickle, so you must find a way to catch their attention and hold it, just the way actors do in plays. And what do you have to do this? Your presence (your body language, your facial expression, the clothes you are wearing [see Chapter 9]), your personality, your use of language or "voice" (see Chapter 2), your style, and your knowledge. Really great speakers can hold an audience's attention for a long time without using PowerPoint or other audio-visual aids. And that's because an audience feels that what the speaker has to say is important and useful.

We will understand public speaking to involve a person speaking directly to an audience that ranges from a relatively small number of people at a club meeting or a classroom to a large member of people in an auditorium, a presentation that may also be carried to millions of people in a television audience and giving a prepared talk, speech, or lecture that is continuous—that is, that lasts for a decent amount of time. When the president of the United States gives his State of the Union address, he is in a large room, speaks for around an hour, and, at the same time, millions of people are watching him

Semiotics of Love Poster

carefully on television and listening to what he says on the radio. Most of the time we can assume that public speaking involves face-to-face communication and a prepared, continuous talk.

We must not underestimate the power of a speech. Thus, for example, Barack Obama gave a speech to a Democratic political convention in an auditorium in Boston in 2004 with thousands of people in it; but it was also broadcast on television. And that speech is credited with launching Obama as an important politician and eventually led to him becoming president of the United States.

Aristotle's Rhetoric and Public Speaking

We have already read Aristotle's ideas in his *Rhetoric* about being a persuasive speaker (Chapter 1). He also offers advice on how to give speeches (McKeon 1941:1434–1435):

> In making a speech one must study three points: first, the means of producing persuasion; second, the style, or language, to be used; third, the proper arrangement of the various parts of the speech. We have already specified the sources of persuasion. We have shown that they are three in number; what they are; and why there are only these three: for we have shown that persuasion must in every case be effected either (1) by working on the emotions of the judges themselves, (2) by giving them the right impression of the speaker's character, or (3) by proving the truth of the statements made…. Our next subject will be the style of expression. For it is not enough to know *what* we ought to say; we must also say it *as* we ought; much help is thus afforded towards producing the right impression.

Aristotle goes on, at length, about other related matters, such as how to state one's case (the statement) and prove it (the argument), the power of the human voice, and countless other topics. From Aristotle we get a guide to making speeches:

1. Focus on the argument by working on your audience's emotions, maximizing your status as an authority, and using reason and logic to support your case.

2. Pay attention to style—because the language you use and the way you use your voice will have an important effect on your listeners.

3. Consider the arrangement of elements or topics you deal with in your speech. They should follow upon one another in a logical manner, and your conclusion should leave your audience with a sense of accomplishment—of having learned something of value.

Aristotle is working at a high level of abstraction, here, but he does offer us a guide to public speaking. Of course not all public speaking is based on persuasion, but even in speeches that are basically descriptive or explanatory, you still want to interest and entertain your audience and give them a reason to believe that what you are telling them is truthful and useful to them. It also helps if you have an interesting title for your speech. For example, I titled a lecture I gave in Istanbul a number of years ago "The Semiotics of Love," and that attracted a number of people who were intrigued by my title.

Television Commercials and the Craft of Public Speaking

We can gain some insights into public speaking by taking cues from the best television commercials. These commercials often start in the middle of an action, to make us curious about what is going on, instead of using the old Aristotelian formula of having a beginning, middle, and an end or conclusion. Because audiences don't like being bothered by them, commercials have to attract the attention of television viewers immediately. Then the commercial's goal is to stimulate desire and finally to lead to an action—purchasing some product or service. In speeches, what lecturers seek is "approval" from our audiences—that is, a sense that the time they spent listening to the lecture was worth it. As a public speaker you have an obligation to inform and entertain (in the best sense of the term) your audience. Many communication scholars suggest we think of public speaking as a form of enhanced conversation, though one that is not interactive like personal conversations. That means we should be natural and informal as contrasted with giving an oration.

What I describe as starting in the middle means that when you give a speech, it is important to find something that will make your audience curious about what you are going to talk about. For example, you might start with a story—to get your audience's attention. But it must be relevant to the subject of your talk. Then you can move on to something else, but you must remember to return to the story and tell how it ends and explain how it was relevant. Or you can ask the audience a question to get them thinking or make an outrageous statement that makes them curious.

People are interested in stories and starting with a story is a good way to get an audience's attention. But if your story drags

Levi's Ad
Storyboard

on endlessly, you will lose your audience. You can, of course,
start a story and then move onto something else before returning to the story. And, as I just suggested, the story must be tied
to the subject of your talk.

The Power of Preparation

There are a number of things you can do to prepare for your speech. One thing I would suggest is to be over-prepared. If you practice your speech a number of times, if you tape it and listen to it, if you feel confident about being able to deliver it in a manner that will appeal to your audience, you'll have no reason to worry. It is natural to be nervous before speaking in public. But if you are well prepared and have practiced your speech enough times, you'll be fine. If you're under-prepared, however, you'll have good reason to be nervous.

There are a number of ways you can practice your speeches. First, you can give your speech in an empty room to get a sense of how it flows. Second, you can tape record your speech to see how you sound and to determine whether your organization and choice of language are effective. You can also practice giving it with some friends and see how they respond to it.

Remember to consider your audience's interests and to tie your talk to them. If your focus is on your audience rather than yourself, you'll soon stop thinking about yourself being in front of them and will see yourself as being part of them. And if you can amuse them at the same time you're doing whatever it is you want to do with your speech, all the better.

It is also useful to visualize your presentation in your mind's eye. Imagine yourself in front of your audience giving your speech. Imagine the audience listening to what you have to say and enjoying your talk. Think about when you'll be pausing, what body movements you might want to make, when to give the audience time to respond to any humor in the speech. Over prepare and you'll do well.

Discursive
Speaker

The Need to Focus

It is important to maintain your focus on whatever it is you are talking about. You want to avoid speaking in a discursive style. Discursive speakers digress from the subject of their presentations and talk about all kinds of things tangential or not even related to what they said they would talk about. And often they digress from their digressions. This usually means they lose their audience, who start wondering what's going on.

Keeping focused means that whatever you talk about should be relevant to your main topic. It is also a good idea to be mindful of the flow of your speech. You can also help your audience by giving them transition cues such as, "on the other hand," "in addition," "now we consider," and so on. It is also helps if you inject an element of redundancy in your talks, since some members of your audience may have not paid attention to an important point.

The Art of Being Relevant

Ambrose Beirce, an American humorist known as "Bitter Beirce" because of his hostile aphorisms, described a bore as "someone who talks when you want him to listen." What we learn from Beirce is that people's attention spans are very short and often they may think they know more about what you are talking about than you do. This means we must be relevant to the interests and needs of audiences. We can be relevant when:

1. **We show how what we are talking about will affect them.**

    "I'm going to talk about global warming and the impact it will have on your life and your children's lives. And your grandchildren's lives. The extreme weather we've been experiencing in the United States may be indirectly caused by global warming, and as the icecaps in Greenland melt and the level of the seas rise, in the not too distant future you may find that where you are living will be under six feet of water."

2. **We take advantage of their desire for information of use to them.**

"You can be healthier if you adopt the Mediterranean diet and eat lots of fresh vegetables, such as broccoli and avocados, eat a handful of nuts every day, and use olive oil for your salads. And the wonderful thing about the diet is that it is delicious as well as healthful."

3. **We provide them with information they didn't have.**

"Some adolescents are now sending as many as one hundred text messages a day to their friends. They spend over an hour a day doing so. This means that in the course of a month they send three thousand text messages and spend more than thirty hours doing so. They may be doing physical harm to themselves with repetitive stress injuries, and they also may be doing psychological harm to themselves by distancing themselves from their siblings and parents."

4. **We show relationships between things they didn't recognize.**

"As a result of the popularity of smartphones, the sales of low-end digital cameras have dropped dramatically, and smartphones are also replacing watches for many people. We don't know how many other industries smartphones will disrupt, but there are plenty of presidents of companies that manufacture things that can be replaced by apps on smartphones who have worried looks on their faces."

5. **We offer explanations they find interesting.**

"Freud's theory of the Oedipus complex may explain why children have such powerful hostile feelings toward the parent of the opposite sex when they are young… and sometimes when they are older. His theory about the unconscious also explains why we do things that are irrational and self-destructive. And that is because there is material in our psyches, of which we are unaware, that shapes our behavior."

6. **We are entertaining, which means we may use our own sense of humor or found humor, here and there, in the talk to amuse people.**

"Before I begin my talk on media, I ought to tell you that a reviewer of my book, *The TV-Guided American,* wrote 'Berger is to the study of television what Idi Amin is to tourism in Uganda.' Since he was murdering hundreds of thousands of people at the time, I have to conclude he didn't like my book." Note: I am quoting here from a review of my book. When I use this quotation in lectures, the audience always has a big laugh (since the review is very insulting). This is an example of what we might call "found humor," in which we use something from the press or some other source in a humorous way. It is not a good idea to start speeches with jokes, because your audience may have already heard the joke, may not think it is funny, and you may not tell jokes well. It is much better to create your own humor, using such techniques as: exaggeration, insult, parody, irony, and so on, or use found humor.

7. **We consider our body language and facial expressions when we talk.**

"You may notice I have a smile on my face. Ordinarily, I never smile. In fact, I can't remember smiling more than once or twice in the past ten years. (Exaggeration and victim humor.) The reason I'm smiling is because I just learned I've been awarded…"

8. **We use but don't overuse audio-visual techniques to enhance our presentations. Images, as I explained in my discussion of nonverbal communication, are very powerful.**

You must be judicious with PowerPoint presentations. They are used so often that some companies now prohibit speakers from using presentation media, in part because the speakers often spend their time talking to the images on the screen and not looking at the audience and interacting with it. If you do use presentation software, don't have slides of long passages of words; it is best to have charts, diagrams, and lists that will be useful to you. Make use of the power of images when you use PowerPoint, not the power of words. As I explained earlier, images fascinate people and have the ability to hold their attention.

We do all of the above using, when appropriate, case histories—stories that allow us to keep our audience's interest and, at the same time, teach them something— and, if possible, also entertain them.

The Audience Shapes the Speech

We must remember one of the key rules of public speaking and communication in general: the audience shapes the speech. We have to adapt our talk to the audience we have. Thus, we give different talks to an audience of teenagers than we do to an audience of senior citizens, and the language we use differs when we talk to audiences that are not highly educated and we talk to a room full of professors or people with advanced degrees. In all cases, though, we must assume a certain level of intelligence in our audience and avoid "talking down" to anyone. We use different language, and we adopt a different tone to our talks. Whenever we communicate with others, we have to be able to reach them, and one way we do this is by adopting an appropriate tone and considering their knowledge base. If you are speaking to people who communicate using what Bernstein called "the restricted code," which he described as being the code for working class people and as being grammatically simple, using short sentences and a limited vocabulary, it doesn't make sense to talk to them using "the elaborated code." This doesn't mean you can't deal with complicated topics. It means you have to explain things using relatively simple language.

We must always remember, of course, to avoid language that members of any audience may find distasteful, such as insulting, sexist, racist, anti-Semitic, and other such kinds of speech.

Audiences don't like being insulted (unless it is by a comedian, and even then it is dangerous), and there's no reason to do anything to antagonize your audience when speaking. You should avoid vulgar language and slang and a style that is not appropriate to your audience. Your audience will expect you to be giving your speech and not plagiarizing material from someone else. You can borrow material from others; that's perfectly acceptable. But you must give them credit for it. You should mention the authors and their works that you are using. For example, if you are using material from Clotaire Rapaille on imprinting in children, you should say something like, "As the French psychoanalyst and marketing consultant Clotaire Rapaille wrote in *The Culture Code...*," and then quote him or paraphrase him.

Speaking at Different Levels on the Ladder of Abstraction

When we speak, just as we don't want to talk in a monotone, without ever raising our voice or always speaking softly, we also don't want to stay at the same level of abstraction. By this I mean we should make sure that sometimes we give examples of things we are talking about but also sometimes use abstractions to make generalizations. If we only talk about specific things, our talk has no implications and becomes mired in the particular. If we only talk at a high level of abstraction, we seem to lose contact with reality. So we must learn how to move up and down the **ladder of abstraction**. It was the semanticist S. I. Hayakawa who wrote about ladders of abstraction in his book, *Language in Thought and Action,* which went through many editions. Let me offer an example. My ladder starts at the bottom with Rover and moves up the ladder to kinds of dogs to common pets and, finally, to animals of all kinds.

The Ladder of Abstraction

Five Tips for Giving Interesting Speeches

Philosophers and others have been writing about rhetoric for thousands of years, and there are a huge number of concepts—with Latin names—that make up the field. Thus, rhetoricians talk about "enantiosis," which means "irony," and "Parataxis," which means "placing side by side." And there are thousands of other terms like the ones I've given.

Cicero, one of the great rhetoricians, wrote, in his *De Oratore,* about the "five parts" or rhetoric:

> Since all the activity and ability of an orator falls into five divisions…he must first hit upon what to say; then manage and marshal his discoveries, not merely in orderly fashion, but with a discriminating eye for the exact weight as it were of each argument; next go on to array them in the adornments of style; after that keep them guarded in his memory; and in the end deliver them with effect and charm. (1942:xxxi)

That is, according to Cicero, a speaker must consider:

Inventio	Invention	The content of your speech
Dispositio	Arrangement	How you order the elements in your speech
Elocutio	Style	Your style of speaking
Actio	Delivery	Your use of your voice in speaking
Memoria	Memory	What your audience remembers about your speech

These are the basic components of public speaking and can serve as a kind of summary for you to keep in mind when thinking about your speech. I should add, as a general note, that it is perfectly useful to use the word "I" and personal pronouns like "he" or "she" when you speak. Trying to avoid using "I' and personal pronouns can lead to all kinds of problems and awkward linguistic complications. Using "I" may also help guide you to create a personal style that will make you and your audience more comfortable when you speak.

I offer now five tips, based on the rhetorical principles just discussed, that will help you give strong speeches.

1. Description

This involves how much detail you include in describing things. If you are too general or vague, your audience won't get a good picture of what you're talking about, and if you are too detailed, your audience may lose the thread of your argument or become bored. Think of the difference between saying "I had lunch at Le Meridien" and the kind of description of a typical meal at a good French restaurant found in restaurant reviews in the *New York Times*. In these reviews, the restaurant critics discuss the atmosphere in the restaurant, the foods served, the specialties of the restaurant, the quality of the cooking, what particular dishes taste like, what dishes were successful and what dishes weren't, and all kinds of other things. People prefer detailed descriptions because it gives them a better sense of what you are talking about.

2. Exemplification

This involves giving examples of whatever it is you are talking about, and going from the general to the specific. For example, if you are talking about how the Supreme Court works, you should then discuss some important cases. Exemplification is a way of moving down the ladder of abstraction from animals in general to Rover, your dog.

3. Explanation

Explanation involves telling your audience things like how some process works or why something happened. This can involve explaining something simple, like the way an Espresso machine works, or complicated, like how Obama won the American presidency or how the Supreme Court makes its decisions. If you talk about a theoretical concept, you should show it can be used to explain something. For example, the concept "obsessive compulsive disorder" helps explain why some people wash their hands two hundred times a day.

4. Figurative Language: Metaphor and Metonymy

There are two kinds of figurative language I wish to focus on here: "metaphor" and "**metonymy**." I've dealt with them in many places in the book, but primarily in Chapter 3 in my discussion of semiotic theory. Metaphor, let us recall, is language that uses "is" and compares two things that are alike in some way. It is based on identity. A weaker form of metaphor is called simile and uses "like" or "as" to compare two things. It is based on similarity. For example, to saying "My love *is* a rose" is a metaphor and saying "My love is *like* a rose" is a simile. Metonymy is based on association, which is used to generate meaning. If we want to suggest wealth in a television commercial, we may show someone in a Rolls Royce automobile. A weaker form of metonymy is called synecdoche, in which a part stands for the whole or vice versa. Thus, we say "The White House" to stand for the presidency and the executive part of the government.

What we must remember is that metaphor and metonym are central to our thinking. As George Lakoff and Mark Johnson write in their book, *Metaphors We Live By* (1980:3):

> Most people think they can get along perfectly well without metaphor. We have found, on the contrary, that metaphor is pervasive in everyday life, not just in language but in thought and action. Our ordinary conceptual system, in terms of which we both think and act, is fundamentally metaphoric in nature.

Sometimes something can function both metaphorically and metonymically. Thus, the snake that tempted Eve is both metaphorically a phallic symbol (all snakes are according to Freud) and metonymically something that calls the Garden of Eden to mind.

If people think metaphorically and metonymically (even though most people may never have heard of the terms), it makes good sense to use metaphors and metonyms in your talk. These devices have the power to grab our attention and impress themselves on our memory.

5. Summaries and Conclusions

A summary is a list of all the things you talked about in your speech, given to your audience as an aid to their memory. One of the canons of public speaking is:

"Tell them what you'll tell them,

tell them,

then tell them what you've told them."

But I have suggested that it is a good idea to start in the middle—to get your audience interested—and then tell them what you'll tell them, then tell them what you want to tell them, and then tell them what you told them. If you offer a summary, you can tell them what you've told them.

If, on the other hand, your talk is such that at the end of it you can show where your talk leads and offer a conclusion that is more than just a summary, you'll have offered a much stronger ending to your talk—because your audience will see where your speech has been leading. Your audience will have discovered something and will probably retain the information you provided more than they would if you ended your talk with a summary. You can think of a conclusion as being something like the way a murder is revealed at the end of a mystery. At the end of Agatha Christie's stories with Hercule Poirot, he usually gathers everyone involved in the story together, offers a summary of what happened, and then reveals how the murderer did it and who the murderer is.

Now Go Out and Do It!

It's one thing to learn theories that will help you perform well when public speaking, but all the theories in the world won't help you unless you use them when you give speeches. So it is important that when you practice your speeches, you make sure you've used the material discussed in this chapter to give your speeches richness and personality. Remember, when you prepare for public speaking, if you don't like what you're saying and find your presentation lively and interesting, your audience won't either.

Applications

1. Using the topics discussed in this chapter, find a speech by the president on the internet and analyze it. What techniques does he use to attract attention and maintain the interest of his audience?

2. Analyze Lincoln's Gettysburg Address. Why does this speech play such an important role in American culture and society?

3. Practice a speech in which you deal with topics at different levels of abstraction. What difficulties did you face in doing this?

4. Does oratory still matter, or is it something that is of diminishing importance? Justify your position. How do conversations and orations differ?

CODA

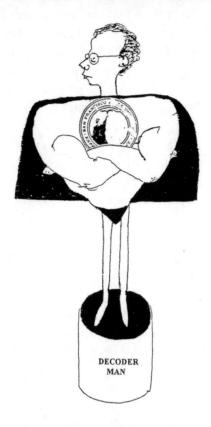

DECODER
MAN

This book is about messages which form the basis of communication. You find the word "messages" being used in many definitions of communication and theories of communication. We are always sending messages about ourselves, though not all of these messages involve words, as studies of body language and facial expression demonstrate. And we are constantly receiving messages sent by others in a variety of ways. I have dealt in this book with many ideas and theories about these messages—each of which tries to help us understand better what communication is and how it works, and the role it plays in our lives and our societies.

In my introduction to this book, I wrote that one goal of this book is to change the way you see the world, and see yourself, one page at a time. To help me do this I have offered a number of quotations from important thinkers about communication that will allow you to see both what their ideas were and how they expressed themselves. You will have read passages from some of the most celebrated theorists—who offer ideas that will help you understand better the process of communication and the complications involved in sending and interpreting messages.

One subtext of this book is that we are seldom aware of the unconscious forces that shape our behavior and, in particular, the way we communicate. Thus, I suggest that though we may not be aware of it, the Bible and certain ancient Greek and Roman myths play an important role in our culture, helping shape everything from psychoanalytic theory to popular culture. I also discuss M. M. Bakhtin's theory of intertextuality, which helps explain not only why our conversations take the shape they do but also the relation of works of art to one another—sometimes borrowing story lines (think "Romeo and Juliet," "West Side Story," and "Shakespeare in Love.") And I have a good deal of material on codes in language, behavior, and cultures. My interest in codes explains my caricature of myself as "Decoderman."

Every idea and theory in this book can play a role in helping you understand how messages work and how they shape our consciousness and affect society. Communication is so interesting because it can be analyzed in so many different ways. Many years ago someone wrote that communication is a field into which scholars from various disciplines wander, hang around for a while, and then leave. Now that we have many schools of communication, we find that a good percentage of the scholars who wander into the field hang around for a long time, and many never leave. What these scholars bring is different theories and methodologies that help us understand how messages function. Thus, Marxist theory has become increasingly important as a means of assessing the role communication plays in politics and the social order. Sociologists have had interesting things to say about genres and the uses and gratifications we obtain from the media. Freud alerts us to the role of the unconscious in our

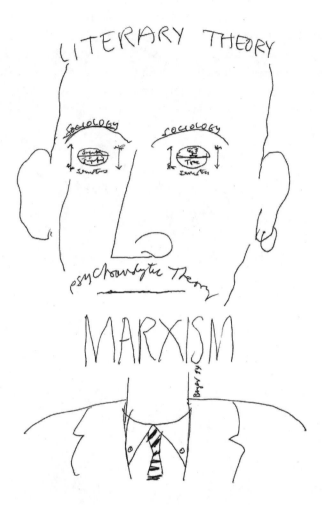

lives and the messages we send and receive. And semioticians teach us how to find meaning in the messages we receive.

After reading this book you will have learned about many aspects of the communication process, how complicated the process of communication is, and how difficult it is to assess its effects. I believe that your exposure to the different thinkers discussed in the book will help you make sense of what is involved in communication and the role it plays in your life.

I've made a number of drawings that I've used in this book and found other images to help illustrate some of the topics I deal with to make *Messages* more visually engaging. Over the course of my career—and I published my first book almost fifty years ago—I've written over 70 books. This book, because it covers so many topics in a limited number of words, has been one of the most difficult books I've ever written. I hope you think it was worth the effort. If you wish to contact me, you can do so at arthurasaberger@gmail.com, but please don't ask me to help you with your course assignments.

GLOSSARY

Aberrant Decoding

This involves audiences interpreting texts in ways that differ from the ways the creators of these texts expect them to be understood. According to Umberto Eco, abberant decoding is the rule, rather than the exception, when it comes to the mass media.

Agenda-Setting

According to agenda setting, the institutions of mass communication don't determine what we think, but do determine what it is that we think about. Thus, they set an agenda for our decision-making and influence our social and political life in important ways.

Alienation

Marx's theory that alienation—a sense of estrangement from others and oneself—affects everyone in Capitalist countries.

Aristotle

Greek philosopher who wrote important works about rhetoric and other aspects of communication. He said art is an imitation of reality (the "mimetic theory of art") and suggested that art functions as a catharsis, relieving people of emotional stress.

Artist

For our purposes an artist is not only someone who does paintings or sculptures or plays a musical instrument, but anyone involved in the creation or performance of any kind of text—especially a mass mediated text.

Audience

We can define audiences of the mass media as people who watch a television program, listen to a radio program, attend a film or some kind of artistic performance (symphony, rock band, and so on). The members of an audience may be together in one room or in many different places.

Basil Bernstein

An English socio-linguist who suggested that there were two codes—the elaborated code and the restricted code—that could be found in English society and were connected to socio-economic class.

Body Language

A form of nonverbal communication in which we send messages to others by the way we use our bodies.

Broadcast

This term is used to deal with texts that are made available over wide areas by using radio or television signals. Broadcasting differs from other forms of distributing texts, such as cable casting, which uses cables, and satellite transmission, which requires "dishes" to capture signals sent by satellites.

Catharsis Theory

Aristotle's notion that our exposure to texts, even if they have violence, is beneficial since it enables us to purge ourselves of powerful emotions.

Class

From a linguistic standpoint, a class is any group of things that has something in common. In social thought, we use the term "class" to refer to social classes, or socioeconomic classes: groups of people who differ in terms of income and lifestyle.

Messages: An Introduction to Communication by Arthur Asa Berger, 221–230.

Class Conflict

Marxist theorists suggest that there is a ruling class which shapes the ideas of the proletariat, the working classes. The history of all societies is based on class conflict, which, Marx argued, will end when class distinctions are erased in communist societies.

Codes

Conventionally, we describe codes as systems of symbols, letters, words, sounds, or whatever that generate meaning. Language is a code. It uses combinations of letters that we call words to mean certain things. The relation between the word and the thing the word stands for is arbitrary, based on convention. In some cases, the term "code" is used to describe hidden meanings and disguised communications.

Communication

For our purposes, communication is a process that involves the transmission of messages from senders to receivers. We often make a distinction between communication using language, verbal communication, and communication using facial expressions, body language and other means of nonverbal communication.

Communications

Communications, the plural of the term "communication," refers to the actual messages, to what is communicated, in contrast to the process of communication.

Concept

Concepts are ideas or notions that are found in theories. For example, the concept "obsessive compulsive" from psychoanalytic theory explains or helps us understand why some people wash their hands two hundred times a day.

Conversations

Are formally structured narrative communications between two or more people that involve turn taking and other rules, most of which exist below the level of our consciousness.

Critical (Marxist) Research

Critical approaches to media are essentially ideological; they focus on the social, economic, and political dimensions of the mass media and the way they are used by organizations and others allegedly to maintain the status quo rather than enhancing equality.

Crowds

Crowds are groups of people who are often swayed by emotions to do things the individuals in the crowd would never do. The French Sociologist Gustave Le Bon wrote a book, *The Crowd,* that is considered a classic of sociological thought.

Cultivation Theory

George Gerbner, who developed cultivation theory, suggests that television dominates the symbolic environment of its audiences and generates false views of what reality is like in television viewers. That is, television "cultivates" or reinforces certain beliefs in its viewers, such as the notion that society is permeated by violence and we live in a dangerous world.

Culture

There are hundreds of definitions of this term. Conventionally, we understand culture to involve the transmission from generation to generation of ideas, arts, customary beliefs, ways of living, behavior patterns, institutions, and values. When we apply the term "culture" to the arts, it refers to "elite" kinds of art works, such as operas, poetry, classical music, serious novels, and so on.

Cultures

I see cultures as collections of codes which tell us what to do in a variety of situations. That is, cultures are collections of codes, most of which exist below the level of our awareness.

Culture Code

A French psychoanalyst and marketer, Clotaire Rapaille, wrote a book, *The Culture Code,* which argues that children are imprinted by the rules and codes of their national cultures between the ages of one and seven. These codes will then shape their behavior when they are adults.

Defense Mechanisms

Freud described defense mechanisms as methods used by the ego to defend itself against pressures from the id (impulsive elements in the psyche) and superego elements such as conscience and guilt. Among the more common defense mechanisms are *repression* (barring unconscious instinctual wishes, memories, and so on from consciousness), *regression* (returning to earlier stages in one's development), *ambivalence* (a simultaneous feeling of love and hate for the same person), and *rationalization* (offering excuses to justify one's actions).

Demographics

The term "demographics" refers to similarities found in selected groups of people in terms of matters such as religion, race, gender, social class, ethnicity, occupation, place of residence, education, and age.

Dialectical Materialism

Marx argues that society shapes consciousness, not consciousness society. This belief is at the center of dialectical materialism.

Dialogism

This theory comes from the writings of the Russian scholar M. M. Bakhtin, who argues that speech is "dialogical," and is based on both what was said before and what will be said in the future. If we apply this theory to texts, we get "intertextuality," which suggests that all texts borrow from one another, sometimes consciously, as in parody, and other times by language or theme.

Digital

What digital systems do, according to Peter Lunenfeld, author of *The Digital Dialectic: New Essays on New Media* (1999:xv) is "translate all input into binary structures of Os and Is, which can then be stored, transferred, or manipulated at the level of numbers or "digits" (so called because etymologically the word descends from the digits on our hand with which we count out those numbers)."

Dr. No

This spy novel by Ian Fleming, and the film made from it, featuring a monstrous Chinese villain, Julius No, is analyzed in many ways in this book.

Egalitarians

One of the four lifestyles discussed by grid-group theorists. Egalitarians stress the ways in which people are similar, try to lift up the downtrodden (Fatalists), and are critics of the two dominant lifestyles—Elitists and Individualists.

Ego

For Freud, the ego functions as the executant of the id. It also mediates between the id (desire) and the superego (conscience, guilt). The ego is involved with the perception and the adaptation to reality.

Elitists

They are one of the four lifestyles discussed by grid-group theorists. Elitists believe in hierarchy in society but also have a sense of responsibility to those who are members of other lifestyles.

Erik Erikson

A psychoanalyst who did a great deal of work with children and adolescents. I used his theories to help explain the importance of smartphones to adolescents.

Ethical Media Criticism

Ethics is the branch of philosophy that involves our sense of what is moral, correct, and good. Ethical critics deal with texts in terms of the moral aspects of what happens in the texts and the possible impact of these texts on those exposed to them.

Ethos

For Aristotle, "ethos" referred to the character and authority of the speaker, which could be used to persuade those listening to him or her. His other two techniques were "pathos," stirring people's emotions, and "logos," logical arguments. It is best, he suggested, to use all three.

Facial Expression

Facial expressions are one of the more important ways in which we communicate nonverbally. According to Paul Ekman, a psychologist who is an authority on the subject, there are eight universal facial expressions and countless others that are not universal. There are forty-three muscles in the face that we use to show emotions.

False Consciousness

In Marxist theory, false consciousness refers to mistaken ideas that members of the proletariat or working classes have about their class, status, and economic possibilities. These ideas help maintain the status quo and are of great use to the ruling class, which wants to avoid changes in the social structure. Marx argued that the ideas of the ruling class are always the ruling ideas in society.

Fatalists

The Fatalist lifestyle is one of the four lifestyles that grid-group theorists claim exist in modern societies. Fatalists are at the bottom of the totem pole and find it hard to escape from their situation. Egalitarians try to help them improve their situation.

Focal Points

In my model, focal points refer to the five areas we can concentrate upon in dealing with mass communication: the art work or text, the artist, the audience, America (or some other country), and the media. All are connected to one another, and we can focus on one or more focal points in doing research.

Formula

A formulaic text, in narrative theory, refers to one with conventional characters and plots with which audiences are familiar. Genre texts, such as spy stories, westerns, sitcoms, detective stories, science fiction, adventures, and romances are highly formulaic.

Gatekeepers

For agenda theorists, gatekeepers are editors and others who determine what stories are used in newspapers or news programs on the electronic media. Gatekeepers determine what news stories we get, but in a broader sense, gatekeepers decide what programs and films we see, what songs we hear, and so on, and in doing so, help set our agendas.

Gender

Gender refers to the sexual category of an individual—masculine or feminine—and to behavioral traits customarily connected with each category. Gender is now considered socially constructed and not "natural," which means people can move from one gender to another.

Genre

The term "genre" is French and means "kind" or "class." A genre refers to the kind of formulaic texts found in the mass media: spy stories, soap operas, news shows, sport programs, horror shows, detective programs, and so on.

Gestures

These are primarily movements we make with our hands when we are speaking with others. We learn gestures as we grow up, and the kind of gestures people make vary from country to country.

Grid-Group Theory

This theory, developed by the English social anthropologist Mary Douglas, argues that there are four "lifestyles" found in modern societies: egalitarians, elitists, individualists, and fatalists. Groups can have strong or weak boundaries and few or many rules. A group can have strong boundaries and many rules (elitists), a strong boundary and few rules (egalitarians), weak boundaries and many rules (fatalists), and weak boundaries and few rules (individualists).

Haptic

A form of nonverbal communication based on touch. It is the opposite of optic, which is based on seeing and scanning.

Hot Media and Cool Media

According to Marshall McLuhan, hot media is characterized by high definition, that is, containing a lot of information, while cool media has low definition, or relatively little information. Movies are hot and television is a cool medium.

Hypothesis

A hypothesis is a guess—a notion that is assumed to be true for the purposes of discussion or argument or further investigation.

Id

Freud developed a theory of the psyche (technically known as his structural hypothesis) in which the "id" is the representative of a person's drives. In his *New Introductory Lectures on Psychoanalysis*, Freud called the id "a chaos, a cauldron of seething excitement." It also is the source of energy, but since it lacks direction, it needs the ego to harness it and control it.

Ideology

In political thought, an ideology refers to a logically coherent, integrated explanation of social, economic, and political matters that helps establish the goals and direct the actions of some group or political entity.

Image

Images are very difficult to define, and there are many definitions of the term in dictionaries. I define an image as a combination of signs and symbols—what we find when we look at things such as a photograph, a film still, a television screen, or a print advertisement. We use the terms also used for mental as well as physical representations of things. Images can have powerful emotional effects on people and have a historical significance.

Individualists

They are one of the four lifestyles discussed by grid-group theorists. Sometimes known as "competitive individualists," their focus is on themselves. This lifestyle is characterized by few rules and weak boundaries, so they are free to pursue their own interests.

Interpersonal Communication

This kind of communication is conventionally understood to involve two people.

Intertextuality

M. M. Bakhtin's theory that all texts are related to one another or "borrow" from one another, sometimes consciously but mostly unconsciously. This borrowing can involve topics, themes, dialogue, images, characters, and so on.

Intrapersonal Communication

We use this term to describe the "talking to ourselves" that we often do when there is something we have to think about. Sometimes this takes the form of imaginary conversations we have with others. I see writing in a journal as a form of intrapersonal communication.

Ladder of Abstraction

The semanticist S. I. Hayakawa suggested that there is a ladder of abstraction, from Rover, our dog, at the bottom, up through pets and other steps to animals. It is a good idea to move up and down the ladder of abstraction when speaking to make your speech more interesting to your listeners.

Language

Languages are unconsciously acquired rules for using words, which are made up of phonemes (the smallest sound units) and morphemes (collections of phonemes) that we form into words and then into sentences. Peter Farb defines language in *Word Play* as a game "similar to other games in that it is structured by rules which speakers unconsciously learn by belonging to a particular speech community" (1976:6).

Lifestyles

The social anthropologist Mary Douglas used this term to describe the four kinds of groups, based on grid-group theory, found in most societies. It also refers, loosely, to the way people live. Grid refers to the number of rules and group refers to the strength of boundaries. There are four possible grid-group combinations leading to four lifestyles.

Marshall McLuhan

He was an important media theorist whose book, *Understanding Media*, contained his theories about the difference between print and electronic media and between hot and cold media, among other things.

Marxism as a Critical Methodology

We have to make a distinction between Marx's economic theories and his other theories, relating to alienation, class conflict, and that kind of thing. Many critics find Marxist concepts useful when they want to analyze mass mediated communication and also to interpret specific texts.

Mass

The term "mass" as in "mass communication" refers to a large number of people who are the audience for some mediated form of communication.

Mass Communication

Mass communication is conventionally understood to deal with the transfer of messages, information, texts, and so forth from a small number of senders to a large number of receivers. This transfer is done through the mass media—newspapers, magazines, television programs, films, records, computers, and now, social media.

Medium (plural: media)

A medium is a means of delivering messages, information, and texts to audiences. One of the most common ways of classifying the media is: print (newspapers, magazines, books, billboards), electronic

(radio, television, computers, CD ROMS, social media), and photographic (photographs, films, videos).

Metaphor

A metaphor is a figure of speech which conveys meaning by analogy. Metaphors are not confined to poetry and literary works but, according to some linguists, are the fundamental way in which we make sense of things and find meaning in the world.

Metonymy

Metonomy is a figure of speech that conveys information by association, and is, along with metaphor, one of the most important ways people convey information to one another.

Models

Models are abstract representations that are used to show how some phenomenon functions. Models are often represented graphically with diagrams. Denis McQuail and Sven Windahl define "model" in *Communication Models for the Study of Mass Communication* as (1993:2) "a consciously simplified description in graphic form of a piece of reality. A model seeks to show the main elements of any structure or process and the relationships between these elements."

Modernism (see Postmodernism)

To understand postmodernism, you have to know something about modernism. The term is used by critics to deal with the arts (architecture, literature, visual arts, dance, music, and so on) in the period from approximately the turn of the century until around the sixties. Some of the more important modernists were T. S. Eliot, Franz Kafka, James Joyce, Pablo Picasso, Henri Matisse, and Eugene Ionesco. The period after Modernism is called Postmodernism.

Morpheme

Morphemes are linguistic units such as words or word elements that cannot be divided into smaller units. Thus the word "dog" is a morpheme, as is the word element "ed" in the word talked.

Nonverbal Communication

We realize now that a great deal of communication comes from nonverbal phenomena. Our body language, facial expressions, style of dress, style of wearing our hair, and gestures are ways of our communicating feelings and emotions (and a sense of who we are) without using words.

Optics

This term focuses our attention on visual phenomena and the way our eyes scan objects. Optics contrasts with haptics, which focuses on touch.

Organizational Communication

The focus in this area of communication study is on the way complex organizations communicate. Organizations are hierarchical in nature and have established ways in which members of the organization communicate with one another.

Pathos

For Aristotle, pathos, in which speakers appeal to our emotions, is one of the most important methods of persuasion.

Phallic Symbol

According to Freud, a phallic symbol is an object that resembles the penis by either shape or function. I suggest that the Washington Monument, built to honor the father of our country, can be seen as a phallic symbol.

Phatic Communication

This term was coined by the anthropologist Bronislaw Malinowski to refer to communication that conveys not information but awareness of someone else. Many scholars believe that texting is essentially phatic.

Phoneme

The term "phoneme" comes from the Greek and means "sound unit." Phonemes are sounds, the smallest significant element of communication.

Play Theory

William Stephenson's book, *The Play Theory of Mass Communication,* argues that the most important function of mass communication is to facilitate play and give people pleasure.

Political Cultures

According to the late political scientist Aaron Wildavsky, whose theories here are based on grid-group theory, all democratic societies have four political cultures and need these four cultures to balance off one another: individualists, elitists, egalitarians, and fatalists.

Popular

This term is one of the most difficult ones used in discourse about the arts and the media. It means appealing to large numbers of people and comes from the Latin term *popularis,* "of the people."

Popular Culture

Popular culture refers to mass-mediated texts that appeal to a large number of people—that is, that are popular. But some mass communication theorists identify "popular" with "mass" and suggest that if something is popular, it must be of poor quality, appealing to the mythical "lowest common denominator." Popular culture is generally held to be the opposite of "elite" culture: operas, plays, serious novels, classical music, and so forth.

Postmodernism (see Modernism)

The term "postmodernism" (sometimes written as post-modernism) means "after modernism," the period from approximately 1900 to the 1960s. Postmodernism is characterized by Jean-Francois Lyotard as "incredulity toward metanarratives" (1984: xxiv). Postmodernists claim that the old philosophical belief systems or metanarratives, such as a belief in progress, that had helped people order their lives and societies are no longer accepted or given credulity. This leads to a period in which, some have suggested, anything goes.

Power

Power can be defined as the ability to implement one's wishes as far as policy in some entity is concerned. When dealing with texts, we use it to describe their ability to generate an emotional impact upon people—readers, viewers, or listeners—which sometimes has social, economic, and political consequences.

Preconscious

In Freud's psychoanalytic theory, the preconscious is the part of their psyches that can be dimly perceived by people. In the iceberg model, it is the part of the iceberg we can see just below the surface of the water. Below it is the unconscious, which we cannot see or access.

Psychoanalytic Theory

According to Freud, the human psyche has what he called an "unconscious," which is inaccessible to individuals ordinarily speaking (unlike consciousness and the preconscious) and which continually shapes and affects our mental functioning and behavior. We can symbolize this by using an iceberg: the tip of the iceberg, showing above the water, represents consciousness. The part of the iceberg just below the surface of the water, which we can dimly make out, represents the preconscious. And the rest of iceberg (about 80 percent of it) represents the unconscious. We are unable to access this area of our psyches because of repression. Psychoanalytic theory also stressed matters such as sexuality and the role of the Oedipus complex in everyone's lives and in our social relations.

Public Speaking

This involves a person speaking to a group, whose size can vary, on some subject in which the speaker has some knowledge or expertise.

Rationalization

A rationalization is a defense mechanism the ego creates to justify some action or inaction. According to Ernest Jones, who introduced the term, it describes seemingly logical and rational reasons that people give to justify behavior that is really caused by unconscious and irrational determinants.

Responsive Chord Theory

Tony Schwartz argues that the function of communication is not to transmit knowledge and information but to "strike a chord" with information already stored in our brains.

Restricted Codes

For Basil Bernstein, "restricted codes" refer to the kinds of langage used by working class people in England that contrast with the "elaborated codes" used by middle class (and above) people.

Role

For sociologists, a role is a way of behaving that we learn in a given society and that is held to be appropriate to a particular situation. We generally play many roles in the course of a day, such as husband (marriage), parent (family), and worker (job).

Sapir-Whorf Hypothesis

This hypothesis argues that language can be seen as working like a prism that helps us make sense of the world. Language is not simply a means of delivering messages but orients us in the world.

Selective Attention (or Selective Inattention)

Psychologists tell us that people have a tendency to avoid messages that conflict with their beliefs and values. One way they do this is by selective attention—avoiding or not paying attention to messages that would generate cognitive dissonance or conflict.

Semiotics (also known as Semiology)

Literally speaking, the term "semiotics" means the science of signs. It comes from *sēmeîon,* the Greek term for sign. A sign is anything that can be used to stand for anything else. According to C. S. Peirce, one of the founders of the science, a sign "is something which stands to somebody for something in some respect or capacity."

Sign

According to Ferdinand de Saussure, one of the founders of semiotics, a sign is a combination of a *signifier* (sound, object) and a *signified* (concept). The relationship between the signifier and signified is arbitrary, based on convention. Signs also can be defined as anything that can be used to stand for something else.

Small Groups

Conventionally, small groups are understood to be made up of between three and twelve people, who have a common purpose and can easily interact with one another.

Socio-Economic Class

Socio-economic class is a categorization of people according to their incomes and related social status and lifestyles. In Marxist thought, there are ruling classes that shape the consciousness of the working classes and history is, in essence, a record of class conflict.

Socialization

This term refers to the processes by which societies teach individuals how to behave: what rules to obey, what roles to assume, and what values to hold. Socialization was traditionally done by the family, by educators, by religious figures, and by peers. The mass media seem to have usurped this function to a considerable degree nowadays, with consequences that are not always positive. Anthropologists use the term "enculturation" for the process by which an individual is taught cultural values and practices.

Spiral of Silence

A German scholar, Elizabeth Noelle-Neumann, developed this theory, which argues that people who hold views that they believe are not widely held (whether this is correct or not) tend to keep quiet, while those who hold views that they think are widely accepted tend to state their views strongly, leading to a spiral in which certain views tend to be suppressed while others gain increased prominence.

Stereotypes

Stereotypes are commonly held, simplistic, and inaccurate group portraits of categories of people. They can be positive, negative, or mixed, but usually they are negative in nature.

Subcultures

Cultural groups whose religious practices, ethnicity, sexual orientation, beliefs, values, behaviors, and lifestyles vary in certain ways from those of the dominant mainstream culture are known as subcultures. In any complex society, it is normal to have a considerable number of subcultures.

Superego

In psychoanalytic theory, the superego is the largely unconscious agency in our psyches related to conscience and morality. It is involved with processes such as approval and disapproval of wishes on the basis of whether they are moral or not, critical self-observation, and a sense of guilt over wrong-doing.

Symbols

In semiotic discourse, symbols are signs whose meanings have to be learned. We can recognize icons (photographs) and make sense of indexical signs (smoke suggests fire), but we have to learn what symbols mean (for example, flags).

Text

We use the term "text" in academic discourse to refer to works of art in any medium, such as plays, novels, comic books, films, television shows, and advertisements.

Texting

Texting generally involves using messaging icons on smartphones to send messages to others. The content of many texts can be described as "phatic" communication.

Theory

As the term is conventionally understood, theories are expressed in language and attempt to explain and predict phenomena being studied. An example would be psychoanalytic theory. Theories differ from concepts, which are parts of theories. An example from psychoanalytic theory would be the unconscious.

Two-Step Flow

This theory comes from research by Paul Lazarsfeld and his colleagues. It argues that there are two steps in the communication process. In the first step, the media influence opinion leaders. In the second step, the opinion leaders, who have high status, influence members of groups of various kinds to which they belong,

Typology

We can define a typology as a classification scheme or system of categories that someone uses to make sense of some phenomenon. Classifications are important, because the way we classify things affects the way we think about them.

Unconscious

According to psychoanalytic theory, our psyches have three levels: consciousness, the preconscious (information of which we are dimly aware) and the unconscious, which is not accessible to us and which comprises most of our psyches. Although we are unaware of it, material stored in our unconscious affects our behavior.

Uses and Gratifications

This sociological theory argues that researchers should pay attention to the way members of audiences use the media (or certain texts or genres of texts) and the gratifications they get from their use of these texts and the media. Uses and gratifications researchers focus, then, on how audiences use the media and not on how the media affect audiences.

Values

Values are understood to be abstract and general beliefs or judgments about what is right and wrong, what is good and bad, that have implications for individual behavior and for social, cultural, and political entities. They play an important role in ethical thinking about the media and other topics. There are a number of problems with values from a philosophical point of view. First, how does one determine which values are correct or good and which aren't? That is, how do we justify values? Are values objective or subjective? Second, what happens when there is a conflict between groups, each of which holds a central value that conflicts with that of a different group?

Violence (Mass-Mediated)

In a study by George Gerbner and Nancy Signorelli, media violence can be defined as (1988, xi) "the depiction of overt physical action that hurts or kills or threatens." In thinking about media violence, we have to recognize that there are a number of different kinds and aspects of violence that have to be considered.

Youth Cultures

Youth cultures are subcultures formed by young people around some area of interest, usually connected with leisure and entertainment, such as, for example, surfing, skateboarding, rock music, or some aspect of computers, games, hacking, and so on. Typically, youth cultures adopt distinctive ways of dressing and develop institutions that cater to their needs.

REFERENCES

ABC News.
abcnews.go.com/Technology/
story?id=3348076

Advertising Education Foundation.
www.aef.com/on_campus/classroom/
speaker_pres/data/1001

Anderson, Craig A. and Brad J. Bushman.
2002.
"The Effects of Media Violence on Society."
Science, March 29, 2002, pp. 2377–2379.

Bakhtin, Mikhail. 1981.
The Dialogic Imagination: Four Essays.
Edited by Michael Holquist. Translated
by Caryl Emerson and Michael Holquist.
Austin: University of Texas Press.

Bennett, Tony and Janet Woollacott.1987.
*Bond and Beyond: the Political Career of
a Popular Hero.*
New York: Methuen.

Berger, Arthur Asa. 1989.
Political Culture and Public Opinion.
New Brunswick, NJ: Transaction Books.

Berger, Arthur Asa. 2005.
*Mistake in Identity: A Cultural Studies
Murder Mystery.*
Walnut Creek, CA: AltaMira Press.

Berger, Arthur Asa. 2012.
Culture Codes.
Mill Valley, CA: Marin Arts Press.

Berger, Arthur Asa. 2014a.
Media Analysis Techniques.
Thousand Oaks, CA: Sage.

Berger, Arthur Asa. 2014b.
*Media and Communication Research
Methods.* 5th edition.
Thousand Oaks, CA: Sage.

Bergson, Henri. 1911.
*Laughter: An Essay on the Meaning of
the Comic.*
London: Macmillan.

Bernstein, Basil."Social Class, Language and
Socialization,"
in Pier Paul Giglioni (ed.), *Language and
Social Context,pp. 175–179.* 1972.
Harmondsworth, England: Penguin.

Bettelheim, Bruno. 1977.
The Uses of Enchantment.
New York: Knopf.

Bottomore, T. B. (ed.) 1964.
*Karl Marx: Selected Writings in Sociology
& Social Philosophy*
New York: McGraw-Hill.

Brantley, Ben.
"Interview with Brendan Jacobs-Jenkins,"
New York Times, March 17, 2014, p. C5.

Brummett, Barry. 2011
Rhetoric in Popular Culture. 3rd edition.
Thousand Oaks, CA: Sage.

Cicero. 1942.
De Oratore.
Translated by E. W. Sutton and H. Rackman.
Cambridge, MA: Harvard University Press.

Cogen, Heidi.
heidicohen.com/social-media-definition/

Cohen, Jodi R. 1998.
*Communication Criticism: Developing Your
Critical Powers*
Thousand Oaks, CA: Sage.

Curteman, Nancy.
Worldpress.com.

Danesi, Marcel. 2002.
Understanding Media Semiotics.
London: Arnold.

DeFleur, Melvin and Sandra Ball-Rokeach.
1982.
Theories of Mass Communication.
4th edition.
New York: Longman.

DeVito, Joseph A. 2011.
Essentials of Human Communication.
7th edition.
Boston: Allyn & Bacon.

Dichter, Ernest. 1960.
The Strategy of Desire.
London: Boardman

Donadio, Rachel.
"When Italians Chat, Hands and Fingers
Do the Talking,"
New York Times, July 1, 2003, p. A6.

Dondis, Donis A. 1973.
A Primer of Visual Literacy.
Cambridge, MA: M.I.T. Press.

Douglas, Mary. 1975.
Implicit Meanings: Essays in Anthropology.
London: Routledge & Kegan Paul.

Douglas, Mary.
"In Defence of Shopping,"
in Pasi Falk and Colin Campbell (eds.),
The Shopping Experience, pp. 15–30. 1997.
London: Sage.

Durham, Meenakshi Gigi and Douglas
Kellner, (eds.) 2001.
Media and Cultural Studies: KeyWorks.
Malden, MA: Blackwell.

Eco, Umberto.
"Towards a Semiotic Inquiry into the
Television Message,"
Working Papers in Cultural Studies
(1972), p. 15.

Eco, Umberto. 1976.
A Theory of Semiotics.
Bloomington: Indiana University Press.

Ekman, Paul and Wallace Friesen. 2003.
*Unmasking the Face: A Guide to Recognizing
from Facial Expressions.*
Cambridge, MA: Malor Books.

Eisenstein, Sergei. 1949.
Film Form.
New York: Harvest/HBJ.

Erikson, Erik. 1963.
Childhood and Society.
New York: W. W. Norton.

Farb, Peter. 1974.
Word Play: What happens When People Talk.
New York: Bantam Books.

Fleming, Ian. 1958.
Dr. No.
New York: Signet Books.

Freud, Sigmund. 1953.
A General Introduction to Psychoanalysis.
Garden City, NY: Permabooks.

Freud, Sigmund. 1901/1965.
The Interpretation of Dreams.
New York: Avon Books.

Gandleman, Claude. 1991.
Reading Pictures, Viewing Texts.
Bloomington: Indiana University Press.

Gerbner, George.
"Liberal Education in the Information Age."
Current Issues in Higher Education,
1983–1984, pp. 14–18.

Giglioli, Pier Paulo, (ed.) 1972.
Language and Social Context.
Baltimore: Penguin Books.

Gladwell, Malcolm. 2002.
The Tipping Point.
Boston: Back Bay Books.

Goffman, Erving. 1972.
Relations in Public
New York: Harper & Row.

Gombrich, E. H. 1960.
Art and Illusion.
New York: Pantheon.

Grotjahn, Martin. 1966.
*Beyond Laughter: Humor and the
Subconscious.*
New York: McGraw-Hill.

Hall, Edward T. 1969.
The Hidden Dimension.
Garden City, NY: Anchor Books.

Hall, Stuart, (ed.) 1997.
*Representations: Cultural Representations
and Signifying Practices.*
London: Sage.

Kaiser Family Foundation.
"Media Use Over Time Among All 8- to
18-year Olds."
www.kff.org/entmedia/upload/8010.pdf

Katz, Elihu, J. G. Blumler, and M. Gurevitch.
"Utilization of Mass Communication by the
Individual,"
in G. Gumpert and R. Cathcart (eds.),
Inter/media, p. 215. 1979.
New York: Oxford University Press.

Key, Wilson Bryan. 1973.
Subliminal Seducation: Ad Media's
Manipulation of a Not So Innocent America.
New York: Signet Books.

Klapp, Orrin E. 1969.
The Collective Search for Identity.
New York: Holt, Rinehart and Winston.

Lakoff, George and Mark Johnson. 1980.
Metaphors We Live By.
Chicago: University of Chicago Press.

Lazere, Donald.
"Mass Culture, Political Consciousness
and English Studies,"
College English 18 (1977), pp. 755–756.

Le Bon, Gustave. 1960.
The Crowd.
New York: Viking Press.
Originally published in 1895.

Lesser, Simon. 1957.
Fiction and the Unconscious.
Boston: Beacon Press.

Linton, Ralph.
"100 Percent American,"
The American Mercury, 40 (1937),
pp. 427–429.

Marx, Karl. 1964.
Selected Writings in Sociology and Social
Philosophy.
Edited by T. B. Bottomore and M. Rubel.
Translated by T. B. Bottomore.
New York: McGraw-Hill.

Mashable.
mashable.com/2014/03/05/
american-digital-media-hours/

Matsumoto, David, Mark G. Frank and
Hyi Sung Hwang, (eds.) 2013.
Nonverbal Communication: Science and
Applications.
Thousand Oaks, CA: Sage.

McCombs, Malcolm and Donald Shaw.
"Structuring the 'Unseen Environment.'"
Journal of Communication, Spring (1976),
pp. 18–22.

McKeon, Richard, (ed.) 1941.
The Basic Works of Artistotle.
New York: Random House.

McLuhan, Marshall. 1965.
Understanding Media: The Extensions of Man.
New York: McGraw-Hill.

McQuail, Denis. 1994.
Mass Communication Theory: An
Introduction. 3rdedition.
Thousand Oaks, CA: Sage.

McQuail, Denis and Sven Windahl. 1993.
Communication Models for the Study of Mass
Communication.
New York: Longman.

Messaris, Paul. 1997.
Visual Persuasion: The Role of Images in
Advertising.
Thousand Oaks, CA: Sage.

Miller, Vincent. 2011.
Understanding Digital Culture.
Thousand Oaks, CA: Sage.

Mirzoeff, Nicholas. 1999.
An Introduction to Visual Culture.
London: Routledge.

Musil, Robert. 1965.
The Man Without Qualities.Vol. 1.
New York: Capricorn.

Noelle-Neumann, Elizabeth.
"The Spiral of Silence: A Theory of Public
Opinion."
The Journal of Communication, Spring
(1974), pp. 44–51.

Ornstein, Robert. 1972.
The Psychology of Consciousness.
San Francisco: W. H. Freeman.

Peirce, Charles Sanders.
Quoted in Zeman, "Peirce's theory of signs,"
in T. A. Sebeok (ed.), *A Perfusion of Signs,*
pp. 22–39. 1977.
Bloomingon: Indiana University Press.

Pew.
"The Web at 25 in the U.S."
www.pewinternet.org/packages/the-web-at-25/

Piddington, David. 1963.
The Psychology of Laughter: A Study in Social Adjustment.
New York: Gamut Press.

Pines, Maya.
"How They Know What You Really Mean,"
San Francisco Chronicle, October 13, 1982,
p. G1.

Pinsker, Joe.
"Punctuated Equilibrium."
Atlantic, July/August 2014.
www.theatlantic.com/magazine/archive/2014/07/
punctuated-equilibrium/372291/

Potter, W. James. 2008.
Media Literacy. 4th edition.
Thousand Oaks, CA: Sage.

The Prisoner. 1967–1968.
UK: ITC Entertainment.

Rapaille, Clotaire. 2006.
The Culture Code.
New York: Broadway Books.

Richardson, Laurel.
"Narrative and Sociology,"
Journal of Contemporary Ethnology (1990),
p. 118.

Rieff, Philip, (ed.) 1963.
Freud: Character and Culture.
New York: Collier Books.

Riessman, Catherine Kohler. 1993.
Narrative Analysis.
Thousand Oaks, CA: Sage.

Saussure, Ferdinand de. 1966.
Course in General Linguistics.
New York: McGraw-Hill.
Originally published in 1915.

Sapir, Edward.
"The Status of Linguistics as a Science,"
Language, 5(4), pp. 207–214.

Scholes, Robert. 1974.
Structuralism in Literature: An Introduction.
New Haven, CT: Yale University Press.

Schwartz, Tony. 1974.
The Responsive Chord.
Garden City, NY: Doubleday.

Sebeok, Thomas A., (ed.) 1977.
A Perfusion of Signs.
Bloomington: Indiana University Press.

Solow, Deanna D. 2014.
The Rhetorical Power of Popular Culture: Considering Mediated Texts.
Thousand Oaks, CA: Sage.

Stephenson, William. 1967.
The Play Theory of Mass Communication.
Chicago: University of Chicago Press.

Toastmasters International
www.toastmasters.org/tips.asp

Turkle, Sherry.
Appearance on National Public Radio show "Fresh Air."
www.npr.org/2012/10/18/163098594/in-
constant-digital-contact-we-feel-alone-
together

University of Wisconsin.
ethicsjournalism.wisc.edu/resources/
ethics-in-a-nutshell/

USA Today.
www.usatoday.com/story/news/
nation/2013/09/16/mass-killings-data

Walsh, David F.
"Subject/Object,"
in Chris Jenks (ed.),
Core Sociological Dichotomies,
pp. 275–298. 1998.
London: Sage.

White, Donald.
"Office Life: Executives Can Lose by a Hair,"
San Francisco Chronicle, December 20, 1980.

INDEX

Names

Topics

ABOUT THE AUTHOR

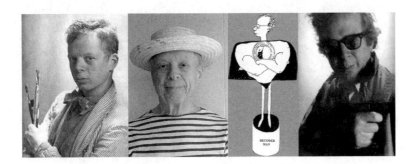

Arthur Asa Berger is professor emeritus of Broadcast and Electronic Communication Arts at San Francisco State University, where he taught between 1965 and 2003. He graduated in 1954 from the University of Massachusetts, where he majored in literature and philosophy. He received an MA degree in journalism and creative writing from the University of Iowa in 1956. He was drafted shortly after graduating from Iowa and served in the U.S. Army in the Military District of Washington in Washington DC, where he was a feature writer and speech writer in the District's Public Information Office. He also wrote about high school sports for the *Washington Post* on weekend evenings while in the army.

Berger spent a year touring Europe after he got out of the Army and then went to the University of Minnesota, where he received a Ph.D. in American Studies in 1965. He wrote his dissertation on the comic strip *Li'l Abner*. In 1963–64, he had a Fulbright to Italy and taught at the University of Milan. He spent a year as visiting professor at the Annenberg School for Communication at The University of Southern California in Los Angeles in 1984 and two months in the fall of 2007 as visiting professor at the School of Hotel and Tourism at the Hong Kong Polytechnic University. He spent a month lecturing at Jinan University in Guangzhou and ten days lecturing at Tsinghua University in Beijing in Spring, 2009. He spent a month in 2012 as a Fulbright Senior Specialist in Argentina, lecturing on semiotics and cultural criticism.

He is the author of more than one hundred articles published in the United States and abroad, numerous book reviews, and more than 70 books on the mass media, popular culture, humor, tourism, and everyday life. Among his books are *Bloom's Morning, The Academic Writer's Toolkit: A User's Manual; Media Analysis Technique; Seeing is Believing: An Introduction to Visual Communication; Ads, Fads And Consumer Culture; The Art of Comedy Writing;* and *Shop 'Til You Drop: Consumer Behavior and American Culture.* Berger is also an artist and has illustrated many of his books.

He has also written a number of comic academic mysteries, such as *Postmortem for a Postmodernist, Mistake in Identity, The Mass Comm Murders: Five Media Theorists Self-Destruct,* and *Durkheim is Dead: Sherlock Holmes is Introduced to Sociological Theory.* His books have been translated into German, Italian, Russian, Arabic, Swedish, Korean, Turkish, Farsi, and Chinese, and he has lectured in more than a dozen countries in the course of his career.

Berger is married, has two children and four grandchildren, and lives in Mill Valley, California. He enjoys travel and dining in ethnic restaurants. He can be reached by e-mail at arthurasaberger@gmail.com.